...e verses of Mark

SOCIETY FOR NEW TESTAMENT STUDIES
MONOGRAPH SERIES

GENERAL EDITOR
MATTHEW BLACK, D.D., F.B.A.

ASSOCIATE EDITOR
R. McL. WILSON

25

THE LAST TWELVE VERSES OF MARK

THE
LAST TWELVE VERSES
OF MARK

BY

WILLIAM R. FARMER

Professor of New Testament
Perkins School of Theology, Southern Methodist University
Dallas, Texas

CAMBRIDGE UNIVERSITY PRESS

Published by the Syndics of the Cambridge University Press
Bentley House, 200 Euston Road, London NW1 2DB
American Branch: 32 East 57th Street, New York, N.Y.10022

© Cambridge University Press 1974

Library of Congress Catalogue Card Number: 73-89003

ISBN: 0 521 20414 3

First published 1974

Printed in Great Britain
at the University Printing House, Cambridge
(Brooke Crutchley, University Printer)

PERITIS SCRIPTURARUM
ATQUE AMICIS PERITORUM

E. C. COLWELL

J. JEREMIAS

C. F. D. MOULE

CONTENTS

CONTENTS

PREFACE

This monograph is offered in response to an observation made by Professor Kenneth Clark in his presidential address to the Society of Biblical Literature, 30 December 1965, at Vanderbilt University, published in *JBL* (March 1966), 1–16. In that address Professor Clark drew attention to 'a most significant event of our day', 'the publication of the N.T. in English bearing the mutual approval of the Protestant National Council of Churches and the Roman Catholic Church'. Professor Clark then undertook to review the alterations that were made in the RSV as it was modified into the RSV CE. He disapproved of the restoration of 'the *pericope adulterae* to its traditional position within the Gospel of John', but immediately went on to say: 'On the other hand, the restoration of the traditional ending of Mark is a wholesome challenge to our habitual assumption that the original work is preserved no further than 16: 8.' Professor Clark expressed the opinion that Justin, Irenaeus, Tatian, and the earliest translations – Latin, Syriac and Coptic – all witness for inclusion, and concluded: 'Witnesses both for and against the CE restoration as genuine are early and impressive, and we should consider the question still open.' More recently Eta Linnemann in 'Der (wiedergefunde) Markusschluss', *ZThK* 66 (1969), 255–87, has argued that Mk. 16: 15–20 is original to Mark, even if 16: 9–14 is not. Linnemann's article did not appear until after this study was completed, so that no special reference to her work is contained herein. In general it may be said that Linnemann's criticisms of Morgenthaler's statistical arguments against the authenticity of Mk. 16: 15–20 are supported by the analysis of Morgenthaler's work made independently and presented in Part Two of this monograph. But both Linnemann and Morgenthaler deal with only a part of the relevant evidence. The relatively complete treatment of the phenomena presented in Part Two lends some support to Linnemann's division of 16: 9–20 into two parts, but not so as to preclude 16: 9–14 from being a part of the original text of Mark. Her own hypothesis that the original text of Mark is preserved in Matt. 28: 16–17 would seem to be unnecessarily complex, though by no means impossible. Kurt Aland, in 'Der wiedergefundene Markusschluss? Eine methodologische Bermerkung zur textkritischen Arbeit', *ZThK* 67 (1970), 3–13, criticizes Linnemann's work. Aland in 'Bermerkung zum Schluss des Markusevangeliums' in E. Earle Ellis and Max Wilcox (eds.), *Neotestamentica et Semitica: Studies in honour of Matthew Black* (Edinburgh, 1969), pp. 157ff., argues for a consideration of the shorter ending as original. G. W. Trompf notes some objections to this view in 'The first resurrection appearance and the ending of Mark's Gospel', *NTS* 18 (1972), 329, n. 5. Jeanine Depasse-Livet in a dissertation for the Licentiate in Theology at the University of Louvain in 1970 ('Le Problème de la Finale de Marc: Mc 16: 8, Etat de la Question') has provided a review of the debate concerning the authenticity of Mark 16: 9–20, pp. 9–36. This monograph also contains a valuable bibliography of studies of the subject (especially full on twentieth-century literature), pp. x–xxi, and gives an inventory of manuscripts, pp. 2–8. Walter Schmithals, in 'Der Markusschluss, die Verklärungsgeschichte und die Aussendung der Zwölf', *ZThK* 69 (April 1972), 379–411, argues that Mark 16: 15–20 belonged originally to an ending of a source that was used by the Evangelist, i.e. that these verses are to be dated earlier than the composition of our canonical Mark.

I am immeasurably indebted to Ernest Cadman Colwell, M. Jack Suggs and Ernest Tune for their constructive criticism of this work as it passed through its several revisions. I wish to thank Page Thomas for his assistance in the preparation of the index and the preparation of the bibliography, and for checking the bibliographical references and conforming them to the style recommended by the Cambridge University Press. H. K. Moulton was kind enough to give the typescript of the main body of the text a careful reading, for which I am very grateful.

My thanks to Vella Massey and Anne Norris for typing and checking a difficult manuscript. I gratefully acknowledge the assistance of Sergio Bontempi, Biblioteca Apostolica Vaticana, in locating and arranging for the photographing of the Mai fragment.

WILLIAM R. FARMER

ABBREVIATIONS

ANF	*The Ante-Nicene Fathers*
HTR	*Harvard Theological Review*
JBL	*Journal of Biblical Literature*
JHS	*Journal of Hellenic Studies*
JTS	*Journal of Theological Studies*
Mai, *NPB*	Mai, A. (ed.), *Nova patrum bibliotheca*
Mai, *SVNC*	Mai, A. (ed.), *Scriptorum veterum nova collectio e vaticanis codicibus edita*
NPNF[1]	*Nicene and Post-Nicene Fathers of the Christian Church,* 1st series
NPNF[2]	*Nicene and Post-Nicene Fathers of the Christian Church,* 2nd series
NTS	*New Testament Studies*
PG	*Patrologia graeca,* ed. J. P. Migne
PL	*Patrologia latina,* ed. J. P. Migne
RB	*Revue Biblique*
SNT	*Supplements to Novum Testamentum*
TU	*Texte und Untersuchungen*
YSR	*Yale Studies in Religion*
ZThK	*Zeitschrift für Theologie und Kirche*

ΕΥΣΕΒΙΟΥ ΠΡΟΣ ΜΑΡΙΝΟΝ

[Quaestiones ad Marinum]

The part of the Mai fragment attributed to Eusebius upon which much of the argumentation concerning the authenticity of the last twelve verses of Mark is based will be found reproduced on the following pages (i.e. pp. xiii–xvi). The text concerned is preserved on fols. 88–9 of Codex Vat. Palat. vol. 220, and is here reproduced to exact measurement. Because of larger outer and lower margins it was not practical to show the full size of the Codex without reducing the reproduction. The actual folio measurements are 24·1 to 24·2 cm high and 18·0 cm wide. Photographs were made available through the courtesy of the Vatican Library. See pp. 3–5 for further bibliographical details and for John W. Burgon's translation of the relevant parts of this text.

ϛ

φοβηθέντεϲ οἱ μάγοι ἀπὸ τῆϲ ὁδοῦ οἱ ἰδίαν. ὁ δ᾽ ὁμοῦ τὸ παιδίον
μετὰ μαρίαϲ τῆϲ μηβ αὐτοῦ· καὶ πεϲόντεϲ. προϲε-
κύνηϲαν αὐτῷ. καὶ αὐτὴ μὲν ἡ περὶ τὴν λῆψιν ἀθ᾽ ὅμτο
λύϲιϲ· ταύταϲ οἱ δὲ ἡμῖν ἢ ὅπωϲ ταῦτ᾽ ἀνδρῶν
καὶ φιλοπόνωϲ ταῦτ᾽ ἃ ὀφαγϲ. γηηϲίαϲ ὅμτα
δὲ γμ̄ατα διαδόϲεωϲ ἁμαλίαϲ τὸ : ‐

✠   ΕΥΣΕΒΙΟΥ ΠΡΟϹ ΜΑΡΙΝΟΝ :

Τὸ μὲν ἡ τοῖϲ θο πη ὅυϲτοιϲ ὁυ ἁγϲ οἷϲ περὶ τὴν
ἀρχὴν ἀπόρου μόνον ζητημάτων καὶ λύϲεων.
δι᾽ ὃ τ πω μ ἡλιϲ ἢ διὰ προτέρομ ϲυγγράμματα.
παρ᾽ ἡμῖν τὰ μ ὅταϲ παρ ὅτι θεων. ἃπϲ τὰ προϲ τοι
τὸ ϲ τῶν αὐτῶν πάντοϲ τὸ τοῖϲ πᾶϲι ζητου μ
μα· τὰ λαπουτ ἡ ϲ τ οῦ θῦ ιου λϲ διὰ το μ ϲ ὅμ ἐπὶ
τα μ τῶν ἐπὶ τοῦτο ἡμᾶϲ παρορ μἡϲαϲηϲ μαρῖνε
ἡ ὅ τιμιώτατε μοι καὶ φιλοπονώτατε· ἡ ὅϲ τ πϲ
δὴ τὸ πρῶτον :‐

✠   πωϲ παρὰ μὲν τῶ ιμαθθλίω ὀψὲ ϲαββάτων
        φαίνεται ἐγηγερμένοϲ ὁ ϲηρ· παρὰ δὲ τῶ
        μάρκω ιπρωϊ τῆ μιᾶ τῶν ϲαββάτων :

Τούτου δὴ τμ αμ ὅ ἡ λύϲιϲ· ὁ μὲν γὰρ τὸ ιϲ φαϲαι
ὁ αὐτὸ τὴν τοῦτο φάϲκουϲαν περὶ μοτοι ἡ αὐθέωϲ.
ὅ ποιαμ μὴ ὁ γ ἃ παϲι μαυτὴ ὅ δρ ὅϲθαι τοῖϲ ἁμη
γραφοιϲ τὸν κατὰ μαρ ιϲ ου ἁγϲ λίου· τὰ γο ὑμ
αιμ ρι ιμ τῶμ ἀμπ γραφομ. τὸ τόϲοϲ περι γραφϲ
τὴ ὁλϲ ταυτὸμ μαρ ιϲ ον ἱ ϲ τορίαϲ ὑπ τοῖϲ ϲ λογοιϲ πᾶϲ
ὁ δρ ὁϲ θτο ϲ μ θαμι σιου ταῖϲ γ υναι ξὶ ιϲαὶ ὁ ρ φλω
τοϲ αὐταῖϲ μὴ φοιϲ ὁϲθϲ · ιν ζὴ πῷ τὸ τομ μο ϲα
ρ ημ ὁμ ιϲαὶ τοῖϲ οβ ἡϲ ὃιϲ ὠπὶ λϲα· ιϲαὶ ἀμ ούϲαϲαι

σφ...ον· καὶ οὐδ' ἐπὶ οὐδὲν ὅτι... πον· οὐ θ... ω... τοῦ γὰρ
ἐπί... ὑπὸ γὰρ σχεδὸν ἐν ἅπασι τοῖς... ἀντιγράφοις
τοῦ κατὰ Μάρκον εὐαγγελίου πέρι γέγραπται τὸ
τέλος· τὰ δὲ ἑξῆς σπάνια... ὅτι... ἐν ἄλλοις ἐμπε-
ριφερόμενα πέρι... ἀνάγκη· καὶ μάλιστα εἴπερ ἐμπε-
χοι ἐν ἀντιλογίᾳ... ἐπὶ τὴν τῶν ... τὸ μεν μαρ-
τυρίαι· ταῦτα μὲν οὖν ᾧ ποιεῖται παρὰ τοῦ ...μενος
καὶ πάντα... αἱ ῥοῦν πέρι τὴν ὅραω τὴν... ἄλλος δὲ
τις οὐ δ' ὁτιοῦν τολμῶν... ἀθετῶν τὸ μὲ... ποσσ... ἐν
τῇ ιτων εὐαγγελίου γραφῇ φερομένων διὰ τῆ...
ἐμαι... τὴν ἀνάγνωσιν... καὶ ἐν ἑτέροις πολ-
λοῖς εἰς ἀντιγράφοις παρὰ τὸ εἰωθὸς ... γὰρ τὰ...
ἄλλων ταύτῃ διὰ ... ἢ ὅτι ... ἢ ἐπὶ ταύτην πα... τοῖς
... καὶ εὐλαβῶν ... μηδὲ... καὶ διὰ τοῦ δὲ
τοῦ μέρους συγχωροῦμένου ... καὶ ἢ ... τρος· προσ...
... τὸ μὲ... ὧδε ἐπεὶ μὲν ἐν τὸ ... ἀναγνωσμάτο Ο
... οὖν δ... τοῖς μὲν τὴν τοῦ λόγου διάνοιαν· οὐ καὶ ἐν
ῥοι μὲν αὐτὴν ἐν ἅπα... τοῖς... τοῦ ματθαίου ὁ τε
σαββάτων... καὶ γὰρ... τὸν σαβ... λεγομένοις· τὸ γὰρ
... δὲ πρωῒ τῇ μιᾷ τῶν σαββάτων... καὶ πα τὸν
μάρκον· μετὰ δὲ τὸ... ἀναγνωσόμεθα· καὶ μὲ...
τοῦτο... δὲ ὑπὸ στίξομεν· καὶ τὴν διάνοιαν
ἀφοριοῦμεν τῶν ἑξῆς ἐπιλεγόμενων· ὥστε τὸ μὲν
... ἂν· καὶ τὴν παρα... σημαίνοι... τε σαββά-
των· τὸ τε γὰρ ... λεγον τὸ... τὸ δὲ ἑξῆς ἑτέραν δη-
... ὑπὸ τὸ πρωῒ... καὶ συναπτομένῃ τοῖς ἐπιλεγο-
μένοις· πρωῒ γὰρ τῇ μιᾷ τῶν σαββάτων· ὅ φαμεν... ἡμέ-
ρα τῇ μιᾷ... τοῦτο γοῦν ἐδήλωσε· καὶ ὁ

ἰωαννην πρωῒ καὶ αὐτὸσ τῆι μιᾶι τοῦ σαββάτου
ὡσ φθᾶ αὐτὸμ τῆι μα(γ)δαλινῇ ἣ μαρτυρίασ· οὗτοσ
οὖ μίαν παρ αὐτοῖ μαρ κωσ πρωῒ ἐφανη αὐτῆι
ὁ υπρωῒ ἁμαται· ἀλλα πολὺ πρότερον κατα τὸν
ματθαῖο μὸ τὸ τοῦ σαββάτου· τὸ τόγαρ ἁμαται
ἐφανη τῆι μαριαι· οὗτο τὸ· ἀλλα πρωῒ· ὡσ σωρι
σασθαι ὅμ τούτοισ καιρουσ δύο· τὸν μὲν γαρ τῆσ αμα
σασθαι· τὸν δὲ τὸ τοῦ σαββάτου· τὸν δὲ τῆσ ὀψρσ
ὡσ ἐφανφασ· τὸ μ πρωῒ ὀψ ἐγρατὸ νὸ μαρ κωσ ἐφανη·
ὁ καὶ μετὰ διαστολῆσ ἀναγνωστ ἐον· ἁμαται δὲ·
ἐφ ταυ ὑποστιξαμετα· τὸ ὀψ λοφῆ τὸμ πρωῒ τῆι μιᾶ
τὸν σαββάτου ἐφανη μαρία τῆι μα(γ)δαληνῆι·
ἀφ ἧσ ἐκβεβλήκει ἑπτα δαιμόνια· :–

X   πῶσ κατὰ τὸν ΜΑΤΘΑΙΟΝ ὀψὲ ϲΑΒΒΑΤΩΝ
    ΗΜΑΓΔΑΛΗΝΗ ΤΕΘΕΑΜΕΝΗ ΤΗΝ ΑΝΑϲΤΑϲΙΝ
    ΚΑΤΑ ΤΟΝ ΙΩΑΝΝΗΝ Η ΑΥΤΗ ΕϲΤΩϲ ΑΚΛΑΙΕΙ
    ΠΑΡΑ ΤΩ ΜΝΗΜΕΙΩΙ ΤΗΙ ΜΙᾼ ΤΟΝ ϲΑΒΒΑΤΟΥ:

Β υδὲ μ(ὲ)ν ζη τη θη κ καὶ αὐτοῦ τοῦ τόπου ϙ τὸ ὀτὸ
    σαββάτον μλ τήν ἀωρῖν ὥραν τὴν μ φα την
    ἡμέρα τοῦ σαββάτου λέγεσθαι ὑπολα μοι μόν οσ·
    τηρ ἐ ὑποφλή φασὶν· ἀλλα τὴν ρα δι καὶ ὸ τὸ τὴν μ
    κτοσ τῆσ μ γα τὸ σαββάτου· οὗτω γαρ καὶ ὁ τὸ τῆσ
    ὥρασ φασ θα μὲν λε γει· καὶ ὁ τὸ τοῦ καιροῦ· καὶ ὸ τὸ
    τῆσ χρ φασ οὗ τῆι φ ἀωρα ανδ κ ἰωπ τὸ· οὐδε τὸν μ φ
    τα κ λ οὐδ υσμεα χρονον· τὸ δὲ σφοδρα καιρα γον
    τούτωσ λ ἡμῖ νομ τα τῶι τρόπωι· ὁ θ θμνο σ αωρδη
    ὁρ μλημ ὑμον αὐτὸσ ἑαυτὸν ὁ ματθαῖοσ μ φα τὸ ὀτὸ
    σαββάτου. ὡσ ἡ γαρ τῆι ἑπ φα φοσ κουσ ηι φ κοῖ·

ημα διὼ ὥρα τῆι λοιπῆ πομ μὴ δὴ ὑποφαμ ρουση· και
ἐπι φωσκουση τὴν κυριακὴν ἡμ ὅραν. η πο λη
ὁ τε και πορρω λοιπον ὅταν μου σαπο μ σαμματων·
λες γεται δε ὁ τε του σαμματου παρ ὁ που ὅρ μ
ν συ σαμτος τὴν γραφην· ὁ μ βη γαρ συ αγ ε χι τιθε
ματθαιος. ὅμα αι δη γρο τη π παρ ὅδος κ ὁ τ τον
αγ ετιον· ὁ δε ἐσι τὴν ὁπ ην ωομ θ ωμ τὴν μεταια
λο μ αὐτο. τὴν ἐπι φωσ λίου σαν ὁ ὅραν ὁ σ τὴν κυρι α
κὴν ἡμ ἐραμ ὁ τε σαμματοσ ομ προσ ε ων· ὁ αγ θ
τον αὐτον σχεδον μο σ οσθαι καιρον. η τὸ μ σφοδρα
αγ μος παρ απ ὁ ισ συα γ οη α ιο διαφορα ισο νο
μα σι τῆς ἡμ λογον· μη δ ην π δ γα θ ὅρ αμ ματθαιον
ὅρ λι οται. ὁ τε δε σαμματων τῆι ἐπι φωσ λίουση
ὁ σμι αν σαμματων ηλ θο μαρια η μα δα λη η
και η αλλη μαρια θεωρ ησαι τον τα φον· ι ω σ αμ μου
θ η ω σ αντος τη δ εμ αι των σαμματων ὅρ χεται μα
ρι α η μα δα λη η προ ι ο τ ομ ἡμ ε ον ετι ου σησ
σκοτιασ· πλαπη λιωσ γαρ ὅρα ις και τον μ αυτον λ η
λω μ χρονον δ γα θοροισ ρ ημα σι ομ μ ματθαιος
ὁ τε αντι του κυραδ ρομ κ αι ὁ τε τηι ου λι πος ομ ομα
σαω προσ ι ὁ δη ὅρ μὴ ν συ ο μ ωη γα ε το σκε πι ασ
ου σησ· ι να μη πισ τομ ὅρ θρον λε α μ αυτο μ ύπο
ρα μοι ω σιασ ὁ ματθαιος τ ὁ τε σαμματων. ι να
μὴ τὴν απορι η λι ωραν γομι οσ ε τι σ λε σ οσθαι
προσ ο θη λισ· τ ὁ τηι ἐπι φωσ λίουση ε σ μ αν σαμ
ματων· ἐπι και αλ ε ρι μο δσ ουτο σ σαμματου ε ηπω
τὴν ὁ λαν μη πισ τὴν απ ὅραν ὑπο ρα μοι λι σ οσθαι
τὴν μετα λι ου δυ σ μασ. αλ λα σαμματων μ θ λοι κ

PART ONE
THE EXTERNAL EVIDENCE

I. THE WITNESS OF EUSEBIUS

(a) *Quaestiones ad Marinum*

In 1825 Cardinal Angelo Mai edited fragments believed to be from a lost work of Eusebius.[1] The lost work in question in its full form seems to have consisted of three books or parts; the first two addressed 'to Stephanus' in which difficulties at the beginning of Mark are discussed; while the third, addressed 'to Marinus', relates to difficulties in Mark's concluding chapters. The plan was, first, to set forth a difficulty in the form of a question, and then to propose a solution for it.

The text published by Mai seems to be only a highly condensed version of the original work. It bears the title: *An Abridged Selection from the 'Inquiries and Resolutions in the Gospels' by Eusebius*. By whom this abridgment was made is not known. But it must have been made by the fifth century, because Jerome knew it in this abridged form. It would seem that the first two books or parts of the original work are represented in what has come down to us by sixteen 'Inquiries', and proposed solutions, addressed 'to Stephanus'. The third and concluding book or part is represented by four more 'Inquiries and Resolutions', this time addressed 'to Marinus'.

However, this third book, which is generally referred to as 'Quaestiones ad Marinum', is believed to have contained, if indeed it did not entirely consist of, 'Inquiries, with their Resolutions, concerning the death and resurrection of the Divine One [Jesus]', and there is evidence indicating that chapter 13 of this work related to Simon the Cyrenian bearing Jesus' cross. It should be apparent, therefore, that the four questions in the text published by Mai represent only a small selection from the latter portion of a much larger work.

---

[1] These fragments are preserved in a manuscript in the Vatican library, designated as 'Codex Vat. Palat. ccxx pulcherrimus, saeculi ferme x'. The fragment in question extends from fol. 61 to 96 of the Codex. The 1825 edition can be found in Mai, *SVNC*, I, 1–101. These same fragments were republished by Mai in 1847 in his *NPB*, IV, 219–309, and it is to this later edition that scholars generally refer, cf. *PG*, XXII, 937–58, 1016.

3

It is the first of these four questions in the text published by
Mai that draws our attention.[1]

How is it, that, according to Matthew [28: 1], the Saviour appears to have
risen 'in the end of the Sabbath'; but, according to Mark [16: 9], 'early
the first day of the week'?

This difficulty admits of a twofold solution. He who is for getting rid of
the entire passage, will say it is not met with in *all* the copies of Mark's
Gospel: the accurate copies, at all events, making the end of Mark's
narrative come after the words of the young man who appeared to the
women and said, 'Fear not ye! Ye seek Jesus of Nazareth', etc.: to which the
Evangelist adds, – 'And when they heard it, they fled, and said nothing to
any man, for they were afraid.' For at those words, in almost all copies of
the Gospel according to Mark, comes the end. What follows, (which is met
with seldom, [and only] in some copies, certainly not in all,) might be dispensed with; especially if it should prove to contradict the record of the other
Evangelists. This, then, is what a person will say who is for evading and
entirely getting rid of a gratuitous problem.

But another, on no account daring to reject anything whatever which is,
under whatever circumstances, met with in the text of the Gospels, will say
that here are two readings, (as is so often the case elsewhere); and that *both*
are to be received, – inasmuch as by the faithful and pious, *this* reading is not
held to be genuine rather than *that*; nor *that* than *this*.

Well then, allowing this piece to be really genuine, our business is to
interpret the sense of the passage. And certainly, if I divide the meaning
into two, we shall find that it is not opposed to what Matthew says of our
Saviour's having risen 'in the end of the Sabbath', (for it was *then* that He
rose); and all that comes after, expressive as it is of a distinct notion, we shall
connect with what follows; (for it was '*early*, the first day of the week', that
'He *appeared* to *Mary Magdalene*.'). This is in fact what John also declares;
for he too has recorded that 'early, the first day of the week', [Jesus]
appeared to the Magdalene. Thus then Mark also says that He appeared
to her early: not that He *rose* early, but long before, (according to that of
Matthew, 'in the end of the Sabbath': for though He *rose* then, He did not
appear to Mary then, but 'early'). In a word, two distinct seasons are set
before us by these words: first, the season of the Resurrection – which was
'in the end of the Sabbath': secondly, the season of our Saviour's Appearing
– which was 'early'. The former, Mark writes of when he says, (it requires
to be read with a pause) – 'Now, when he was risen'. Then, after a comma,
what follows is to be spoken – 'Early, the first day of the week, He appeared
to Mary Magdalene, out of whom He had cast seven devils.'

[1] The exact reference is as follows: 'Quaestiones ad Marinum', Mai, *NPB*,
IV, 255–7. All that has been said thus far has been gleaned from the more
complete but somewhat excited introduction to the matter which was
given by John W. Burgon in *The Last Twelve Verses of the Gospel According to
Mark* (Oxford, 1871), pp. 41–4. In an appendix to that book on pp. 265–6
Burgon reprints the Greek text as published by Mai, and on pp. 44–6 he
gives his translation of Mai's text, which is reprinted here.

Before attempting to evaluate this text for the question concerning the last twelve verses of Mark, it is important to bring into view what is found at the beginning of the answer to the following question. The second of the four questions Marinus asks is: how is it that (according to Matthew) Mary Magdalene beheld the risen Lord at the end of the Sabbath, while (according to John) the same woman on the first day of the week stood crying by the tomb? The answer to this question is prefaced by the following words:

These places of the Gospels would never have occasioned any difficulty, if people would but abstain from assuming that Matthew's phrase (ὀψὲ δὲ σαββάτων) refers to *the evening of the Sabbath-day* [i.e. Friday night, the Sabbath commencing at sunset on Friday]: whereas, (in conformity with the established idiom of the language) it obviously refers to an advanced period of the ensuing night. The self-same moment therefore, or very nearly the self-same, is intended by the Evangelists, only under different names: and there is no discrepancy whatever between Matthew's – 'in the end of the Sabbath, as it began to dawn toward the first day of the week,' and John's – 'The first day of the week cometh Mary Magdalene early, when it was yet dark.' The Evangelists indicate by different expressions one and the same moment of time, but in a broad and general way.[1]

If one assumes that Eusebius is responsible for this observation (and he would seem to be if he is the author of any part of Mai's text), how can one understand Eusebius to be also responsible for the views expressed in the answers to the preceding question? For these are not two unrelated questions, but two questions caused by what is ostensibly the same misunderstanding. That misunderstanding has to do with how to interpret Matthew's phrase ὀψὲ δὲ σαββάτων. According to Eusebius it can be understood to mean in a broad and general way the same time as 'early the first day of the week'.

Once this view of ὀψὲ δὲ σαββάτων is accepted, the answer to the first question of Marinus would be: 'The discrepancy is only apparent. The text of Matthew, properly understood (i.e. understood in conformity with the established idiom of the language), places the resurrection of Jesus during the night that came between the Sabbath and the morning of the first day of the week, and, therefore, if "early on the first day of the week" is taken to refer to a time before the break of dawn on Sunday

---

[1] Cf. Burgon, *Last Twelve Verses*, pp. 46–7, 266. Burgon has really only given the substance of the text which is prolix. Cf. *PG*, xxii, 940ff.

(as John 20: 1 shows it can be taken) then the resurrection according to Mark could be understood to have taken place the same time as is attested in Matthew.'

This suggests that the answers given to the first question, answers which seem to be uninformed by the interpretation of ὀψὲ δὲ σαββάτων given in the second, were conceived originally by someone else, and, before being incorporated into the text that has come to us, enjoyed an existence independent of the exegetical tradition which informs the formulation of the answer given to the second question in Mai's text.

The first question is answered according to an understanding of ὀψὲ δὲ σαββάτων which acknowledges a clear and serious time-discrepancy between the time indicated for the resurrection by Matthew and the time indicated by 'early on the first day of the week' in Mark. This time difference can be accounted for in two ways according to the text of Mai: one can reject the passage in Mark as unauthentic, or one can punctuate Mark's text so that 'early on the first day of the week' refers to Jesus' appearance to Mary, while ἀναστάς is left to refer back in time to an antecedent resurrection which could have taken place at whatever time is indicated in the text of Matthew. By contrast the recognition, found in the opening words of the response to the second question, that ὀψὲ δὲ σαββάτων is commensurate with 'early on the first day of the week', renders the first solution to the first question of Marinus entirely unnecessary, and renders the second solution to that question invalid, since it seems to presuppose a view of Matthew's use of ὀψὲ δὲ σαββάτων that is subsequently repudiated. This clearly shows that the text of Mai is not a simple straightforward consistent homogeneous attempt to deal with a particular set of critical problems. It is more like a developed compilation in which earlier more or less effective answers to various closely related questions have been edited and reissued by someone (possibly Eusebius) without reworking the whole according to any single and consistent set of critical presuppositions.

As confirmation of this interpretation of the matter we may turn to Augustine's *The Harmony of the Gospels*, where in Book III he treats at great length and in wearisome detail the many alleged discrepancies between the resurrection narratives of the Gospels. Augustine elaborates on the importance of recognizing that Matthew's expression, 'the end of the Sabbath', means Saturday night. Once having set forth the basis for this understanding of Matthew's expression Augustine proceeds to deal with the manifold problem of harmonizing the resurrection accounts of Matthew, Mark and Luke and John. But he makes no mention of the discrepancies between Matthew and Mark and Matthew and John to which the first two questions of Marinus draw attention – and for a very simple reason. His work (at least at this point – and in contrast to the text of Mai) is a self-consistent, critical achievement worked out on the basis of a single set of presuppositions – including the same understanding of the meaning of Matthew's expression ὀψὲ δὲ σαββάτων which is found in the text of Mai at the beginning of the response to Marinus' second question.

The import of all this is that if Eusebius is giving expression to his own critical judgment in saying that these questions from Marinus proceed from a misunderstanding of the text of Matthew, then the recorded discussion of the discrepancy between Matthew and Mark preserved in Mai's text in which reference is made to the existence of manuscripts which end at ἐφοβοῦντο γάρ must be older than Eusebius, and must have come to him as a twofold solution which was worthy of perpetuation in spite of the fact that Eusebius himself, on the basis of his own convictions, regarded the question as misconceived from the start. This does not settle the question whether Eusebius can be cited as a witness for omitting the last twelve verses of Mark. There is still the matter of the Eusebian canons in which there appears to have been no provision for these verses in Mark. This matter will be dealt with later. At the moment it is only necessary to recognize that this text of Mai, if cited as a witness regarding the authenticity of Mk. 16: 9–20, must be cited in a way that recognizes the complexities and subtleties of the matter.

Indeed even confining ourselves to the first question, we can see that the framework of that twofold response belongs to the world of hypothetical rhetoric, so that it is very difficult to determine whether there was any intention on the part of the author (whether he be Eusebius or some earlier authority) to commit himself one way or the other.

The use of the potential optative in the opening and closing sentences of the paragraph concerned would seem to indicate this. Let us step back from the text and delineate the literary structure of the response.

First comes the introductory statement: 'This difficulty admits of a twofold solution.' Then follows a relatively well-balanced exposition of the twofold solution. Both parts of this twofold answer are introduced by parallel and properly co-ordinated introductory sentences, whose essential grammatical kinship can be seen in translation only when this formal parallelism is kept in view: 'On the one hand, he who rejects this passage might say that it is not recorded in all the copies of the Gospel according to Mark...' 'On the other hand, anyone who on no account dares reject anything...which is recorded...says that here are two readings...and that *both* are to be received...'

The adequacy of the dialectical character of the twofold response in Mai's text can be measured by the extent to which the intended reader is thereby armed to meet sceptical criticism of the Gospel from whatever direction. We may make explicit what is implicit in the text in the following way: 'If you or your inquirer are disposed to be agreeable to excluding doubtful passages, then you may find this particular approach effective: ...However, if you or your inquirer are more conservatively oriented, then here is a different way to resolve the difficulty.'

It will be instructive at this point both to compare and contrast this twofold formulation with one of its parallels in the particular literary tradition in which it stands – namely that of patristic treatment of textual variants in the scriptures.

This particular parallel is taken from one of Origen's homilies.[1] Origen, in considering a passage from Jeremiah (15: 10–19), comes to a point in the text where he finds two variant readings (verse 10). He proceeds:

The text has two readings. For, on the one hand, in most copies it runs, 'I was of no help (ὠφέλησα), nor did any man help me.' But, on the other hand, in the texts which are most accurate and agree with the Hebrew, it stands, 'I was not in debt (ὠφείλησα), neither was any man indebted to me.' We must then both explain the text that is current and usually commented on in the churches, and also not leave unexplained the text based upon the Hebrew.

Origen then gives an exegesis of the text found in the majority of manuscripts, after which he writes:

But a further interpretation also is necessary, because the most accurate

---

[1] *In Jeremiam Homilia* 14, PG, XIII, 403–27.

copies read thus: 'I was not in debt, neither was any man indebted to me.' Let us then interpret the passage in this form.

Then comes an exegesis of the text known to Origen, but not current nor usually commented on in the churches – a text which followed the Hebrew and in his judgment was more accurate than that of those found in most manuscripts.

This is far from an exact parallel to the situation represented in Mai's text. There was no Hebrew original to appeal to in the case of Mark, and the nature of the textual variants is as different as can be imagined – i.e. in the one case the presence or absence of an iota, but in the other, the inclusion or omission of a passage of several verses.

Notwithstanding these and obvious formal differences there are formal similarities that are important for a proper understanding of the text of Mai. In the case of the textual variant in Jeremiah we find a scriptural exegete taking the initiative to bring to the attention of the faithful the existence of a reading presumably unknown to them. There is no doubt that this is the reading he prefers. He clearly states that it is the more accurate and wants his readers to realize that it has the authority of the more original Hebrew text lying behind the Greek. If this were a commentary of Origen rather than a homily we might expect him to indicate more explicitly to his readers his reasons for regarding the one text as more accurate than the other. It is easy to see that ὠφείλησα, the original and correct translation of the Hebrew, has been misunderstood or miscopied in Greek producing a text with ὠφέλησα, which, while it makes sense and can be interpreted in an edifying way and was found in most of the manuscripts being used in the churches, simply cannot have been original for the simple reason that one cannot reverse the transmissional sequence. One cannot imagine the Hebrew text as established by a careful examination of the oldest copies available to Origen[1] concurring with a change which so obviously belongs to the transitional history of the Greek texts.

There is no problem thus far in our understanding the context in which Origen stood. We can see that he faced a situation in which his own judgment went against the received practice of

---

[1] Origen's first-hand experience with the Hebrew manuscripts, like his topographical researches in Palestine, marks him out as the first proponent of environmental research – this the father of exegetical and systematic theology in the church!

the churches and we learn that, faced with such a problem, he both took seriously the possibility that the text current in the churches was correct and then proceeded to take seriously the possibility that another reading was correct. Unlike Marcion, who in a like situation simply would have rejected the majority reading, Origen carefully took both into account. This is perfectly consonant with what we can learn from Origen's text-critical and exegetical practices throughout his life.[1]

We should acknowledge, therefore, that Origen was capable of having originated the basically conservative, but not uncritical, twofold formulation we find embedded in the response to the first question of Marinus in Mai's text. And the fact that Eusebius was an admirer of Origen and a proponent of the great Alexandrian's exegetical and textual tradition is also consonant with this redactional analysis of Mai's text.

But such specific attributions are not essential to a proper understanding of Mai's text. It is enough to know where we are in the exegetical history of the church. We are in the school of Origen (sometime in the third or fourth century) where it was recognized that the differences among manuscripts of vital importance to the church had become great – both through the unintentional carelessness of copyists and through the intentional initiative of some who interpolated and omitted as they saw best. Even though Origen in his Commentary on Matthew (15: 14) complained about this situation, he himself, on occasion, was quite capable of advocating changes in the texts of scripture.[2] Bruce Metzger has noted that in the majority of cases where Origen mentions a variant reading in the text of the New Testament he merely observes that some copies present a different reading, without indicating which he prefers. Metzger regards this apparent nonchalance as 'tantalizing' and contrasts it with Origen's procedure in dealing with the Greek text

---

[1] Frank Pack, 'The methodology of Origen as a textual critic in arriving at the text of the New Testament' (unpublished doctoral dissertation, University of Southern California, May 1948), pp. 54–232.

[2] This matter is carefully reviewed by Bruce M. Metzger as far as it affects New Testament texts in 'Explicit references in the works of Origen to variant readings in New Testament manuscripts', *Biblical and Patristic Studies in Memory of Robert Pierce Casey*, eds. J. N. Birdsall and R. W. Thomson (Freiburg, 1963), pp. 78–95. It is treated fully by Pack, 'Methodology', pp. 54–232.

of the Old Testament. Metzger finds the primary reason for this difference in the circumstance that with the Old Testament Origen had a Hebrew original against which the Septuagint and other Greek versions could be compared, whereas any such norm by which to judge the validity of variant readings in the New Testament texts was lacking. For this reason, suggests Metzger, 'Origen hesitated in most instances to pass judgment upon the genuineness of this or that reading.' However, as Metzger notes, in several instances, Origen does indicate his preference.[1]

In the five instances listed by Metzger where Origen indicates his preference for a particular New Testament textual variant, he *four times sides against* the readings of the majority of manuscripts in current use in the churches known to him and *once with* the majority reading.

His preference for the minority reading which we see him making in his treatment of the problem of textual variants in Jer. 15: 10 is in keeping with what seems to have been his tendency in those few instances where we have good reason to think we can detect his preference in treating New Testament variants.

What can be learned about the textual situation that is presupposed in the answer given to the first question of Marinus in Mai's text? And what, if anything, can be learned about the preference of the person responsible for formulating that twofold response? If he preferred one solution to the other, it probably would have been the second. Pride of place in matters of this kind is usually given to the voice which is allowed to speak the final word. Whether we can make anything out of the fact that the optative is used in framing the first solution and the indicative the second is not clear. But the fact that the first solution is both begun and ended in the optative mood suggests that there is a condition to be fulfilled before one would appeal to the fact that some copies of Mark end at ἐφοβοῦντο γάρ – that condition is that the person concerned would be disposed to reject the passage. This whole matter is made clearer if we compare and contrast the way in which the first paragraph begins and ends with the way in which the second paragraph begins and ends:

[1] Metzger, 'Explicit references', pp. 93–4.

On the one hand he who rejects this passage *might say* that it is not recorded in all the copies of the Gospel according to Mark... These then are the things which *might be said* by whoever would dismiss and altogether do away with a superfluous problem. On the other hand, he who is ill disposed toward rejecting anything recorded in the text of the Gospel *says*: 'Here are two readings, (as is so often the case elsewhere) and *both* are to be received – inasmuch as by the faithful and circumspect *this* reading is not held to be genuine rather than *that*; nor *that* than *this*.'

However, even from this understanding of the text published by Mai, it is clear that some credence must be given the statements that there were copies of Mark in the ancient church, many of them, which ended with ἐφοβοῦντο γάρ. No matter how hypothetically the first answer is framed, it remains incredible to think that the statements about how manuscripts of Mark ended had no basis in fact. What that basis may have been, however, is not easy to ascertain. It is difficult, for example, to take *all* the statements which are placed on the lips of the typical or representative person who is disposed to reject the passage in Mark (whether because he tends on principle to reject doubtful passages, or for some other reason) as based on fact. For, when he is represented as saying that what follows ἐφοβοῦντο γάρ in the Gospel of Mark is 'met with seldom', though that fits with the preceding 'almost all copies', it conflicts somewhat with what is clearly implied in the words which follow, which state that the verses concerned are met with '[only] in some copies', and more sharply with what is implied in the qualifying statement 'certainly not in all'.

Since we have Mark preserved in ℵ and B without any of the verses concerned, there is no difficulty in believing that these verses in the days of Eusebius and before were 'certainly not [found] in all' copies of Mark. That these verses were absent from some copies of Mark, and that in certain locales the majority of the copies of Mark in general circulation ended at ἐφοβοῦντο γάρ, would seem to be the minimal factual basis for the statements placed on the lips of our imagined proponent of excision.

But it is highly improbable that the last twelve verses of Mark were 'met with seldom' in copies of Mark circulating throughout the *whole* of the ancient church. For we cannot imagine the earliest translations – Latin, Syrian, and Coptic – the lectionaries of the church, and Tatian's text all possessing these disputed verses if in fact they were 'met with seldom' in copies of Mark circulating in the churches known to these Fathers. Perhaps that explains why the author of this twofold response, though he seems to have scrupulously avoided passing judgment on the genuineness of either variant reading, has been constrained to use the optative mood in framing the first solution. He seems to recognize that the proponents of omission are capable of making exaggerated claims on behalf of this position.

He apparently is faced with a situation in which the majority of manuscripts in current use in the churches known to him end with ἐφοβοῦντο γάρ. He knows that those copies which are regarded as accurate end this way, and he does not question this judgment. He is faced then with the unusual situation where current local ecclesiastical usage and scholarly judgment seem to be in happy agreement in support of one reading, but where unhappily there is nonetheless another reading which must be taken seriously. Texts which include 16: 9–20 are not defended on any grounds other than the conservative principle of preserving and taking seriously readings that are attested in received copies of the Gospels. It is clear then that our author knew some manuscripts, but not the majority, and not the 'accurate' ones, which included these last twelve verses. Realizing that his questioner is one who knows Mark *with* those verses and wanting to provide him with an answer which will satisfy those who, in spite of objections that can be raised against their authenticity, want to receive these verses, and therefore would not be satisfied with his first solution, and wanting to justify his taking this position seriously, he prefaces his second solution with a rationale for a conservative attitude on this matter. This conservative attitude should not be viewed as rooted in simple obscurantism, but rather as a consequence of a natural reaction against change, in this case a reaction against what were regarded as questionable attempts to produce more accurate copies of the scriptures. Primarily this was not a reaction against truth, but against method. To understand this attitude we need to see the earliest attempts at New Testament textual criticism within the context of a particular school of Hellenistic textual study.

(b) *Alexandrian textual criticism*

We know from some of the quotations Plato and others made from their texts of Homer, that there once existed Homeric manuscripts which included readings which are not found in extant copies. It seems likely that some of these readings were edited out of the manuscript tradition that has been preserved in an attempt to produce more accurate Homeric texts. In any case there was a purifying 'text-critical' project led by Alexandrian scholars which has profoundly influenced the textual history of extant classical manuscripts. The text-critical methods developed in Alexandria in the second century before Christ were later adopted by Alexandrian Christians. The best known example of this influence of Alexandrian text-critical tradition on Christian scholarship is seen in Origen's Hexapla, where, after arranging the text of the Septuagint and that of the Hebrew as well as other Greek translations in parallel columns, facilitating easy comparison, Origen marked passages in the Septuagint which such comparative study indicated were interpolations, and indicated points where omission had been made, utilizing the same critical asterisks and obeli used by those who had sought by comparative manuscript study to produce more accurate copies of the classical Greek texts.[1]

We know of no such project for producing a more accurate text for the New Testament writings. But there is ample evidence that by the time of Eusebius the Alexandrian text-critical practices were being followed in at least some of the scriptoria where New Testament manuscripts were being produced. Exactly when Alexandrian text-critical principles were first used to produce more accurate New Testament texts is not known. However, well before the end of the second century (c. 180), when Pantaenus founded the first known Christian school in Alexandria, the proximity of the great Library of Alexandria and the availability of the text-critical lore of the

[1] Cf. B. H. Streeter, *The Four Gospels* (London, 1924), pp. 111, 122–3. See also J. E. Sandys, *A History of Classical Scholarship*, 2nd ed. (3 vols., Cambridge, 1906–8), i, 105–35 (vol. i only is of the 2nd ed.). It would appear that an adequate description of the critical process employed in formulating the final texts of the Greek writers has yet to be written. E. A. Parsons, *The Alexandrian Library, Glory of the Hellenic World: its Rise, Antiquity, and Destruction* (Amsterdam, New York, 1952), p. 223, writes that such a description would require a treatise of several volumes, and notes that J. W. White 'most properly required 434 pages' to treat the *scholia* of only *one* of the plays of Aristophanes! Nonetheless the principles followed by the Alexandrian text critics are clear enough to warrant the inferences made in this study.

scholars who worked there and made it the great university centre it was created the conditions under which a concern for 'purer' texts of the Christian scriptures was bound to develop sooner or later.[1]

One of the practices of the Alexandrian scholars was to search for the most ancient copies of texts, and then to use these in correcting current copies and in producing new ones. So passages in current copies which were not supported by the most ancient copies were marked for omission, and when a comparison of ancient copies indicated that the current copies were incomplete, they were glossed accordingly, and new copies had these glosses interpolated into the main body of the text.[2]

But Alexandrian scholars were also guided by other principles in making their omissions. And of these one in particular needs to be understood if we are to appreciate the sensitivities of those early Christians who objected to the omission of any passage, however disputed, which was found to be an integral part of a received text. This principle called for the omission of any passage which was regarded as offensive to or unworthy of the gods. In this case it mattered not whether the passage concerned was or was not in the most ancient copies. This is an important point, as we shall soon see. In other words, in addition to the respect for the authority of the oldest manuscripts there was a contemporary theological norm which operated. And classical Greek texts edited in Alexandria were modified accordingly. This was not done irresponsibly. On the contrary, it was done with a conscious recognition of the fact that improved copies of the Greek classics were being made not so much to satisfy the curiosity of the antiquarians as to meet the practical needs of the contemporary reading public.[3]

Zenodotus of Ephesus (c. 325–c. 234 B.C.) was the pioneer in Homeric critical scholarship. His edition was founded on numerous manuscripts. Spurious lines were marked with a marginal obelus. 'His reasons for condemning such lines were mainly because he deemed them inconsistent with the context,

---

[1] Streeter, *Four Gospels*, pp. 111, 122–3.

[2] *Ibid.*, pp. 122–4; Sandys, *History of Classical Scholarship*, I, 120.

[3] However, the most interesting parallel to the textual problem of the ending of Mark, i.e. the problem of the ending of Homer's *Odyssey*, is not a case involving these needs. Cf. J. B. Bury, 'The end of the *Odyssey*', *JHS*, 42 (1922), 1–15.

or unsuited to the persons, whether deities or heroes, whose action is there described.'[1]

Aristophanes of Byzantium (c. 257–c. 180 B.C.) agreed with Zenodotus in obelizing many lines, but he also reinstated, and obelized, many which had been entirely omitted by his predecessor. He seems to have been the first to reject the conclusion of the *Odyssey*, from XXIII to the end. Like Zenodotus he was prone to judge the actions in Homer by contemporary Alexandrian standards, 'and to impute either impropriety, or lack of dignity, to phrases that are quite in keeping with the primitive simplicity of the heroic age'.[2]

Aristarchus of Samothrace (c. 220–145 B.C.) made a careful study of Homeric language, and relied strongly on manuscript authority. In cases of conflicting readings he relied on the poet's usage. 'In contrast with Zenodotus, he abstained from merely conjectural readings, and was even censured by later critics for excess of caution... As a critic he is more sober and judicious than Zenodotus and Aristophanes, but he sometimes lapses, like his predecessors, into an overfondness for finding "improprieties" of expression in the plain and unaffected style of Homer.'[3]

Aristarchus followed Aristophanes in rejecting the present ending of the *Odyssey*. Sometimes the Alexandrians rejected passages without manuscript support for omission. In rejecting the present ending of the *Odyssey* the Alexandrian text critics probably had no manuscript evidence to support omission.[4] This is an important consideration since it establishes the point that the 'philological editorial know-how of Alexandrians', to use the phrase of Colwell (see p. 53), led to the rejection of passages comparable to Mk. 16: 9–20, even when there seems to have been no manuscript evidence to support such rejection. If Colwell is right, that the Beta (B ℵ) text type was produced *in part* by appeal to manuscript evidence, 'but *more importantly* by the philological editorial know-how of Alexandrians [my italics]', then it is not unreasonable to conjecture that omission of Mk. 16: 9–20 may have originated in Alexandria, i.e. was first introduced into the manuscript tradition of Mark under the

[1] Sandys, *History of Classical Scholarship*, I, 120.
[2] *Ibid.*, I, 127. [3] *Ibid.*, I, 133.
[4] Thomas W. Allen, *Homer: the Origins and the Transmission* (Oxford, 1924), pp. 218–19.

influence of Alexandrian editorial practices. For it is not unreasonable to think that once a passage has been designated as a spurious addition, copies of that work will be made in which this passage will be omitted. However, no manuscripts of Homer have come down to us which omit its present ending. Therefore, we lack positive confirmation that Alexandrian editorial practice actually led to the omission of our ending of the *Odyssey*. That is, there is nothing among the known manuscripts of the *Odyssey* like B and ℵ where the ending of Mark is actually missing. But if one or two such early copies of the *Odyssey* were to be discovered, would the omission of the final verses be regarded as evidence supporting the inauthenticity of these verses, or would this omission be regarded as evidence for the influence of Alexandrian text-critical judgment upon scriptorial practice in Egypt and other places influenced by Alexandrian scholarship? This focuses the problem we face in trying to evaluate properly the meaning of the omission of 16: 9–20 from a few early copies of Mark.

(c) *Accurate copies*

What did it mean in the ancient world to designate copies of a work as 'accurate'? The adjective ἀκριβής clearly implies that these copies were the result of careful investigation on the part of qualified experts concerned with the accuracy of the text. However, the surface impression that by 'accurate copies' is meant the earliest, or the most original, is not borne out by a study of the known practice of textual experts in the ancient world.

As we have noted these text critics edited new texts out of old copies, and in so doing they strove to produce improved texts. But some of the practices they followed did not result in producing texts that were closer to the autographs. No doubt the improved texts they produced excluded many textual aberrations found in the extant manuscripts and resulted in restoring well-attested readings that had been accidentally omitted from some copies in careless scribal transmission. To this extent these improved texts approximated to what in the modern period have come to be called 'critical editions'. However, to the extent that phrases and passages which might be deemed 'improper' or 'undignified' were omitted or altered, these 'improved' editions were closer to the original only when the said 'offensive' phrases and passages actually had been introduced by 'impious' men bent on corrupting the morals or beliefs of the readers (to follow the rationalization of the ancient editors). But in every case where the words, expressions, or passages were original, their omission or alteration resulted in the production of an 'improved', but *less original* text. It must be borne in mind that in this sense the 'improved' texts produced by ancient textual experts were also 'censored' texts. The importance of this fact for our problem becomes clear as the grounds for regarding Mk. 16: 9–20 as a passage that could have been omitted with 'good cause' come to the fore. Meanwhile, it is important to realize that ἀκριβής in this context is best rendered: 'carefully edited'. These texts were certainly believed to be more accurate by those who did this editing. But since we cannot accept all the major presuppositions which they allowed to influence their work, we must suspend judgment as to whether the absence of a passage like Mk. 16: 9–20 is primarily due to its absence from some of the earliest and best authenticated manuscripts available to those who produced their 'accurate' copies – or whether this absence is primarily due to other causes. It is worth noting in this connection, as will be shown later (p. 24), that we find ἀκριβής used to refer to copies of Mark which *included* the last twelve verses.

There is the case of Origen's treatment of the textual problem in John 1: 28 where in almost all copies he found the reading 'these things were done in Bethany'. Origen chose Bethabara, a minority reading, because it was the more reasonable and accorded with the facts as he knew them from his own topographical research in Palestine. Later Chrysostom noted the two readings and wrote: 'Many of the more accurate (ἀκριβέστερον) copies have "In Bethabara".'[1]

In this case Origen argued for a reading that went against the best manuscript evidence available to him and to the modern critic. Later Chrysostom referred to manuscripts that had this minority reading as 'more accurate'. Clearly 'accurate' means something like trustworthy in the sense of having been carefully edited on rational principles. Such 'accurate' manuscripts also may have been regarded as the more original. But they were not

---

[1] Cited in C. Tischendorf, *Novum Testamentum Graece*, 8th ed. (2 vols., Leipzig, 1869–72), I, 750.

necessarily the more original, as is illustrated in this instance. In fact Origen acknowledges that 'Bethany' was read by Heracleon and appeared to be an even earlier reading.[1]

It is significant that in Mai's text no special appeal is made on behalf of either reading on the grounds of what stood in the most ancient copies. The assumption that the accurate copies were so called because they were in agreement with the most ancient copies, as we have seen, would not necessarily be the case. In any case, Origen seldom if ever appeals to the authority of the most ancient manuscripts in his discussion of New Testament textual variants.

It would have been uncharacteristic of Origen as an Alexandrian scholar not to have made an effort to consult the oldest manuscripts available to him. But apparently the readings he found in these copies did not commend themselves over those found in other copies. We know that in the case of Old Testament textual variants he gave considerable weight to the readings of the most ancient copies of the Hebrew texts which he could locate. Apparently the situation was one in which in the matter of textual variants there were no completely trustworthy New Testament exemplars known to him. There were simply some copies that were 'truer' or 'better' or 'most accurate', but none that could be commended on the basis that they were the 'most ancient'. This would have been a serious deficiency in the eyes of Alexandrian scholars, and it points up the frustration for Alexandrian exegetes who also wanted to be catholic and wished to base their scriptural interpretations on texts that were uniform and received throughout the church.

From another direction our problem is illuminated by a complaint written near the beginning of the third century by the Roman legal authority Gaius, concerning what had happened to pagan scriptures:

These heretics have audaciously corrupted the divine Scriptures under the pretext of correcting them. In order to convince oneself that this is not a false accusation he has only to glance at their exemplars. Those of Asclepiades are entirely different from those of Theodotus. Their disciples have mutilated these corrected copies which in reality are corrupted copies.[2]

---

[1] Commentary on John 6. 24, *ANF*, IX, 370; *PG*, XIV, 269.
[2] As cited in Eric L. Titus, 'The motivation of changes made in the New Testament text by Justin Martyr and Clement of Alexandria' (unpublished doctoral dissertation, University of Chicago, 1942), p. 2.

2-2

Tertullian could complain of Marcion: 'What Pontic mouse ever had such gnawing powers as he who has gnawed the Gospels to pieces?'[1] We know, however, that many of Marcion's changes were quite justified, granting him his basic dogmatic presuppositions. And this was probably true of much textual change made during the second century. We know that Origen recognized what he believed to be the dogmatic influence of heretics upon copies of the Gospels circulating in the churches,[2] and he himself on occasion was prepared to recommend a variant reading on purely dogmatic grounds.[3]

It was certainly not the general practice of the orthodox to advocate changing the text of scripture on theological grounds. Quite the contrary. But when did orthodoxy in this matter first become powerfully self-conscious? Was it before Irenaeus? And when did it come to dominate textual transmission in the church? Was it before the fifth century?

In rebutting a criticism of Celsus, Origen claimed that Celsus did not observe that Jesus himself is not described as a carpenter anywhere in the Gospels accepted in the churches. But we know that in the most original text of Mark, Jesus is so described. Origen's text agrees with many authorities, such as the Old Latin. But this is a text of Mark that has been assimilated to the text of Matthew (Mk. 6: 3//Matt. 13: 55). Origen in this case is choosing a reading in manuscripts currently accepted in the churches known to him and rejecting a variant reading that was earlier known to Celsus in the second century. This should be

---

[1] *Against Marcion* I. 1, *ANF*, III, 272; *PL*, II, 272.

[2] Pack, 'Methodology', pp. 137–51. Cf. *In Matthaeum Commentariorum Series*, 134: 'I rather believe that the secret enemies of the Church of Christ have altered this phrase.' Said by Origen with reference to the text of Luke which reads: 'The sun was eclipsed.' The purpose of these enemies was to injure the church since they knew that there was no eclipse of the sun recorded for that time. Origen preferred the variant, reading: 'The sun was darkened', which harmonizes with Matthew and Mark. Cf. *PG*, XIII, 1783.

[3] Pack, 'Methodology', pp. 132–3, 149–50. Pack cites Origen's view that 'Jesus Barabbas' in Matt. 27: 16 was a reading in which the heretics had added the name of Jesus. Origen's point against this reading is that the name Jesus could not be applied to evil men like Barabbas. Origen in this case, however, refrained from changing his exemplar, finding a less radical solution in allegory. Cf. *In Matthaeum Commentariorum Series*, 121, *PG*, XIII, 1772–3.

regarded as another case where Origen indicates his preference between variant readings. We see him siding with a variant which presumably originated in a dogmatic tendency to harmonize the texts of the Gospels, and which, in this instance, serves a polemical interest of Christian apology.

The point is that the third and fourth centuries were transitional with regard to attitudes in the church toward changing the texts of scripture. In this period the practice of freely altering the New Testament text was arrested in the church, and the process of correcting changes which had been made in New Testament texts during the second century was begun.[1] But at best these efforts were only partially successful. The instance concerning Origen just cited indicates how difficult it would have been to restore a reading that went against the dogmatic interests of the community, or that was in any way 'unedifying'.

Taking all this into account it is not difficult to understand the reservations of 'pious and faithful' Christians faced by the changing circumstances of a developing situation where it was difficult for anyone but an Origen (and sometimes impossible for him in an altogether satisfactory way) to find his bearings in a sea of textual differences. Eventually local texts emerging under the influence of ecclesiastical authorities would help stabilize the situation, and finally authorized recensions and translations would help solve the problem for the 'pious and faithful'. But in the third and fourth centuries among orthodox Christians there would have been at best an uneasy coexistence between those who advocated adhering only to the readings of what they held to be the 'most accurate' or 'most correct' copies and those who, when faced with variant readings, preferred not to choose between them. This latter attitude was perfectly understandable to a churchman like Origen, and, as we have seen, generally respected by him.

We may now ask whether there is anything in the text of Mai which can help us understand why there were so many copies of Mark circulating in the ancient church which ended with ἐφοβοῦντο γάρ. The answer to this question seems to be 'yes'. For in the text of Mai the judgment that what follows ἐφοβοῦντο γάρ in Mark can be dispensed with is said to be confirmed if 'it

---

[1] Pack, 'Methodology', p. 133.

should prove to contain a contradiction to the testimony of the rest of the evangelists'. It is not affirmed that these verses do in fact contradict the testimony of the other evangelists, but the suggestion is clearly implied that an examination of the matter might show that in fact Mk. 16: 9–20 *does* contain a contradiction of the testimony of one or another of the other evangelists, and *should* this be the case (the optative is used) the grounds for omission would be strengthened thereby.

For the modern critic this seems a strange line of reasoning. It can easily be turned into an explanation for these verses being omitted from copies of Mark in the first place, i.e. the argument would have been: 'if they contain a contradiction to the testimony of the other evangelists, they cannot be authentic and should be omitted'. Following this line of reasoning the explanation for omission would have been: 'these verses obviously have been added by heretics, or by some careless or audacious copyist and cannot have been written by Mark'. All these considerations should be kept in mind as one seeks to understand the apparent contemporary propensity for omission in 'accurate' copies of Mark – for as the question of Mai makes clear the very first words following ἐφοβοῦντο γάρ appear to contain a contradiction to the testimony of one of the other evangelists, i.e. Matthew.

2. THE WITNESS OF JEROME

In a letter written in 406 or 407, Jerome dealt with the same scriptural problems posed by Marinus, though he treats them as questions put to him by a lady of Gaul named Hedibia.[1] Whether Jerome is utilizing another Latin or Greek form of the same text published by Mai, or whether he is modifying this text, it is in any case clear that his letter to Hedibia is secondary to the text attributed to Eusebius. At many points the Latin is no more than a translation of the Greek.

Jerome's procedure in answering such inquiries is outlined in another letter written under similar circumstances:

Being pressed for time, I have presented you with the opinions of all the commentators; for the most part, translating their very words; in order both to get rid of your question, and to put you in possession of ancient authorities

[1] *Epistola* 120, *PL*, XXII, 980–1006.

on the subject...This has been hastily dictated in order that I might lay before you what have been the opinions of learned men on this subject, as well as the arguments by which they have recommended their opinions.

Then after a self-deprecating remark about his own authority, he praises the learning of Origen and Eusebius and the works of many more of his predecessors in scriptural exposition and continues:

My plan is to read the ancients; to prove all things, to hold fast that which is good; and to abide steadfast in the faith of the Catholic Church. I must now dictate replies, either original or at second-hand, to other questions which lie before me.[1]

Thus in his letter to Hedibia, in response to the question about the apparent conflict between Matthew and Mark he writes:

This difficulty admits of a twofold solution. Either we shall reject the testimony of Mark, which is met with in scarcely any copies of the Gospel – almost all the Greek codices being without this passage: – (especially since it seems to narrate what contradicts the other Gospels): – or else, we shall reply that both Evangelists state what is true...For the passage must be punctuated through, – 'When he was risen': and presently after a pause, must be added, 'Early the first day of the week, He appeared to Mary Magdalene...'[2]

What does it mean that Jerome would make use of, and pass on in letter form, the statement that Mk. 16: 9–20 was to be found in 'scarcely any copies' of the Gospel? Is it likely that he would have repeated it, if it was without support in the Greek manuscripts known to him? It seems probable that Jerome knew Greek manuscripts (and possibly Latin ones as well), that omitted the last twelve verses of Mark. But in view of the fact that he included these verses in his Latin translation of the New Testament, and that he treated them as a part of the Gospel in his *Commentary on Mark*,[3] it seems clear that Jerome testifies not only to the existence of the twofold textual tradition in the fifth century but to a responsible scholarly preference for inclusion rather than omission at that time. In view of Jerome's great admiration for the scriptural scholarship of Origen and Eusebius

---

[1] *Ibid.*, 119, *PL*, xxii, 966–80.

[2] Burgon's translations of Jerome have been cited in this section, *Last Twelve Verses*, pp. 52–7.

[3] *PL*, xxx, 642–4.

it seems likely that there was no unambiguous rejection of the authenticity of Mk. 16: 9–20 in that school of scriptural exegesis.

The same twofold response is found in other later patristic writings, including a commentary on Mark attributed to an obscure fifth- or sixth-century writer, Victor of Antioch.

3. A SCHOLIUM TO VICTOR OF ANTIOCH'S COMMENTARY ON MARK

Few commentaries on Mark are known from the early church. This commentary exists in many copies by virtue of the circumstance that it constituted the established commentary on Mark for the later church.[1] Actually it is a catena, rather than a commentary. And though it is usually attributed to Victor of Antioch, in some manuscripts it is credited to other Fathers or is left anonymous.

In spite of the chaotic state of the manuscript evidence for this work on Mark (the texts vary greatly), and the complex question whether the text of Mark presupposed by the original work included 16: 9–20, as well as the question whether the passage including the reference to the twofold response is secondary, there is no doubt that the author of a scholium at the end of this commentary (1) was acquainted with the fact that in very many copies of Mark the last twelve verses were not found; (2) was acquainted with the fact that in very many copies they were found; (3) was persuaded on the basis of his own consideration of the matter that the true text tradition was represented by those manuscripts which did not end with ἐφοβοῦντο γάρ, but went on to include the last twelve verses.

Burgon translates the scholium as follows:

Notwithstanding that in very many copies of the present Gospel, the passage beginning, 'now when [Jesus] was risen early the first day of the week, He appeared first to Mary Magdalene', be not found (certain individuals having supposed it to be spurious), yet we, at all events, inasmuch as in very many we have discovered it to exist, have, out of accurate copies, subjoined also the account of our Lord's ascension (following the words 'for

---

[1] Burgon, *Last Twelve Verses*, pp. 267–90, discusses the history of this text in two appendices. It is also discussed by F. J. A. Hort in the introduction to *The New Testament in the Original Greek* (2 vols., New York, 1881), vol. II, Appendix I, p. 35.

they were afraid'), in conformity with the Palestinian exemplar of Mark which exhibits the Gospel verity.[1]

It is important to note that the statements concerning the existence of very many copies of Mark which *did not* contain the verses in dispute, and the existence of very many copies which *did*, are well attested in the manuscript tradition of this document and are not in doubt. These uncomplicated statements witness unambiguously to a clearly divided textual tradition in the early church regarding the last twelve verses of Mark. Should this scholium be secondary to the original text of the commentary, it would indicate that this divided textual tradition prevailed at least as late as the period when it was added, perhaps as late as the seventh or eighth century.[2] There is no disposition on the part of the author of this scholium to deny the existence of 'very many' copies of Mark which did not contain the verses in question, although in his own judgment these copies were deficient. The author of this scholium then is actually a 'hostile witness', and it is very difficult to avoid the conclusion that at the time this scholium was written and probably also at the time of Eusebius, there were indeed very many copies of Mark like those now preserved for us in B and ℵ with texts ending at verse 8.

At the same time this scholium makes clear what the confusing and baffling statements in Mai's text leave in doubt – namely, the extent to which in the ancient church the last twelve verses of Mark were found in copies of that Gospel. As over against the ambiguous 'met with seldom' – 'certainly not [met with] in all', we have the statement that these verses were found in 'very many' copies of Mark, the term used, πλεῖστος, being the same used to refer to the 'very many' copies which did not record these verses. Allowing for the fact that our author is a 'hostile witness' in these matters, we might conclude

---

[1] Burgon, *Last Twelve Verses*, pp. 64–5. The text of the scholium in most copies ends here but in some it goes on and Burgon's translation of his reconstructed Greek text (this Greek text is printed on pp. 288–9) continues: 'That is to say, from the words, "now when [Jesus] was risen early in the first day of the week", etc., down to "with signs following. Amen".' The Greek text of the whole scholium is critically edited with variant readings by Burgon in Appendix E, pp. 288–90.

[2] (B. F. Westcott and) Hort, *New Testament*, II, p. 35, 'an unknown editor in the sixth or some later, perhaps much later, century'.

that on actual count the number of copies of Mark circulating in his day which did not contain these verses may have exceeded the number which included them. But as we know from the way in which at a later period the manuscript tradition which did not include these last twelve verses became virtually extinct, to count heads at any particular time, whether in the fourth century, or in the fourteenth, is to indulge in little more than a popularity contest. This only puts us in touch with the prevailing practice in the scriptoria of the church in a particular period. Few copies of any ancient book actually in use at any given time were over one hundred years old. What is important in Victor's scholium is the testimony that he was able to discover that in very many copies of Mark these verses were, and in very many copies they were not, recorded. This discovery was probably not made without some research. Victor explicitly tells us that he gave special attention to a particular text tradition preserved in what he designates as a 'Palestinian' exemplar of Mark.

The importance of all this is that it affords the critic some basis for understanding the widespread attestation for the authenticity of the last twelve verses of Mark in the ancient church. If Irenaeus could find these verses in manuscripts of Mark which were received by him as authoritative, we can then understand how he could cite these verses as from the Gospel according to Mark, even though the text tradition preserved by B and ℵ may have been represented in any number of copies of Mark in circulation somewhere in the church at the same time. It would be possible to understand the even earlier witness of Tatian in a similar way (that is, providing a critic should find grounds for thinking that there were manuscripts of Mark as early as the middle of the second century which ended at verse 8).

4. THE WITNESS OF ORIGEN

Origen is sometimes cited as a witness for ending Mark at ἐφοβοῦντο γάρ. This is based on an argument from silence. But it is an argument worth stating. In Augustine's *Harmony of the Gospels* 3. 65–86 the last twelve verses of Mark are treated along with the rest of that Gospel. Mark's account of the post-resurrection appearances of Jesus is listed along with those of Matthew, Luke and John with no indication that there is any question about the authenticity of these verses.[1] By contrast Origen, in dealing with Celsus' criticism of Christian belief concerning the resurrection of Jesus,[2] draws upon the accounts concerning the post-resurrection appearances of Jesus in Matthew, Luke and John, but makes no reference to the account in the last twelve verses of Mark. At one point where Origen is answering Celsus' derisive charge that Jesus showed himself secretly only to one woman – which Celsus could support by appealing to either Mark or John – Origen replies: 'Now it is not true that He showed Himself only to one woman; for it is stated in the Gospel according to Matthew... '[3] Origen makes no reference to either John or Mark at this point. Thus it is not possible to say anything other than that Origen here did have at least the negative opportunity of referring to the last twelve verses of Mark. But note that it was a *negative* opportunity. Origen's silence at this point seems to be no more an argument against the authenticity of Mk. 16: 9–20 than it is against the authenticity of the corresponding section in John. Elsewhere Origen makes reference to the appearances of the risen Jesus recorded in the other three Gospels but never refers to Mk. 16: 9–20. Does his silence mean that he did not know these verses or that he knew them but felt no need to cite them, or that he knew them and did not want to cite them either because he regarded them as unauthentic or because they posed some kind of difficulty?[4]

It is noteworthy that unlike the author of Mai's text, and unlike Augustine in his *Harmony of the Gospels*, Origen in *Contra Celsum* never seems to deal with discrepancies between the Gospel accounts. This is all the more remarkable since one would expect that a critic of Christianity like Celsus, who delighted in drawing attention to the illogical aspects of Christian

---

[1] *NPNF*¹, VI, 210–25; *PL*, XXXIV, 1197–1216.

[2] *Contra Celsum* 2. 56–70, *PG*, XI, 885–907.

[3] *Contra Celsum* 2. 70, *PG*, XI, 905.

[4] G. D. Kilpatrick, 'Three recent editions of the Greek Testament', 2 pts, *JTS*, 50 (1949), 143, comments on Origen's failure to use Mk. 16: 9–20. He refers to *Die Evangelienzitate des Origenes*, 98 (*Texte und Untersuchungen*, 34, 2a (Leipzig, 1909)), where Ernst Hautsch concludes that Origen's text did not contain Mk. 16: 9–20.

doctrine and the incredibility of some of the Gospel accounts, would hardly have missed the opportunity to point out the very kind of discrepancies between the Gospels taken up in the question of Marinus in Mai's text.[1]

In commenting on the text: 'Blessed are the peacemakers',[2] Origen writes that a man becomes a 'peacemaker'

as he demonstrates that that which appears to others to be a conflict in the Scriptures is no conflict, and exhibits their concord and peace...For as the different chords of the psalter or the lyre, each of which gives forth a certain sound of its own which seems unlike the sound of another chord, are thought by a man who is not musical and ignorant of the principle of musical harmony, to be inharmonious, because of the dissimilarity of the sounds, so those who are not skilled in hearing the harmony of God in the sacred scriptures think that the Old is not in harmony with the New, or the Prophets with the Law, or *the Gospels with one another* or the Apostle. But he who comes instructed in the music of God...will bring out the sound of the music of God...For he knows that *all the Scripture is the one perfect and harmonized instrument of God*, which from different sounds gives forth one saving voice to those willing to learn [my italics].

Guided by this principle Origen commented on the text of the scriptures, not devoting himself overmuch to alleged discrepancies, but demonstrating how a true 'peacemaker' plays on the 'one perfect and harmonized instrument of God'. Accordingly the different statements of the respective evangelists concerning the same matters are treated as complementary or supplementary and are never shown to be in conflict.

We know that Origen wrote this commentary in the same period he wrote against Celsus.[3] This suggests that between the time that Celsus wrote *A True Discourse* and Origen wrote his Commentary on Matthew, there had developed a growing

---

[1] Origen seems to have written *Contra Celsum* between 244 and 249, and Celsus seems to have written his work in the period 177–80. Cf. Henry Chadwick (ed. and trans.), *Origen: Contra Celsum* (Cambridge, 1953), pp. xiv, xxviii. See Robert M. Grant, *The Earliest Lives of Jesus* (New York, 1961), p. 59, for the view that Celsus 'took pleasure in pointing out the fact that the various gospels contradict one another'. Although the passage Grant cites in support of this statement (*Contra Celsum* 2. 27) falls short of establishing that Celsus actually drew attention to specific contradictions between the Gospels, it, nonetheless, seems intrinsically probable that Celsus would have delighted in doing this.

[2] Commentary on Matthew, *ANF*, IX, 413; *PG*, XIII, 832–3.

[3] Eusebius, *Ecc. Hist.* 6. 36.

consciousness of the discrepancies between the Gospels. The publication of Tatian's Diatessaron and its use in place of the separate Gospels put the question of the discrepancies between the Gospels in a new light and for the first time provided the basis within the church for acknowledging that this was a problem that needed attention.

In any case Origen's commentaries clearly sidestep the issue on dogmatic grounds. For him there can be no conflict. All that appears as discord is simply a special case of harmony, and it is part of the exegete's responsibility to bring out this hidden harmony. This is one, if not the chief, service rendered the church by the allegorical method of interpreting scriptures.

It is important to note that within the church, the practice of harmonizing, conflating, or combining the texts of the Gospels began very early. We see it as early as Justin, and there is some evidence that Justin made use of the text of an even earlier harmony of the Gospels.[1] Frank Pack has shown that Origen utilized exemplars of the Gospels in which the text of one Gospel had been altered by bringing it into harmony with the parallel text of another. And more important, he shows that Origen himself engaged in such harmonistic conflation.[2]

We know from the apocryphal gospels, as well as from Justin, Tatian and Marcion, and others, that in the second century the texts of the Gospels were altered and combined in many different ways. Origen complained against those who made additions and omissions in the text of the New Testament manuscripts. But that did not keep him from making certain changes he thought were justified. Many, perhaps most, of the changes Origen made in his New Testament texts were influenced by his dogmatic principle of the unity and harmony of scriptures.

Clearly, the second solution to Marinus' question in the text of Mai is in accord with a concern to harmonize the differences between the evangelists. But it must be noted that the first solution served the same purpose, as the words 'especially if it should prove to contradict the record of the other Evangelists'

---

[1] A. J. Bellinzoni, *The Sayings of Jesus in the Writings of Justin Martyr*, *SNT*, 17 (Leiden, 1967), pp. 95, 140–2.
[2] 'Methodology', pp. 182–207.

make clear. Since the harmonizing changes made in Origen's New Testament citations include examples of omission, it seems that, in principle, Origen would not have been opposed to the first solution to the question posed by Marinus, although, to be sure, the second solution would have been in keeping with his moderating disposition as a churchman in such matters.[1]

The first solution may have appealed to Origen as an Alexandrian-trained scholar, whereas the second certainly would have appealed to him as an ecumenically oriented Christian. However, there seems to be no way to proceed beyond these generalizations to any positive statement about what Origen actually thought about the question of the authenticity of Mk. 16: 9–20.

Clement of Alexandria sometimes is cited as a witness for the omission of Mk. 16: 9–20. It is true that, as with Origen, we know of no place where Clement cites or shows acquaintance with these verses. But Clement is equally silent about the last chapter of Matthew, and, therefore, it is difficult to evaluate his silence with regard to Mk. 16: 9–20.

The textual tradition ending Mark with ἐφοβοῦντο γάρ can be traced back as far as the fourth-century manuscripts B and ℵ, and presumably back to their third-century prototype. The intimate agreement between B and P75 in Luke and John, if it can be assumed to have extended to Mark, would carry us back to a second-century prototype. But that such a conjectural precursor for B and P75 omitted Mk. 16: 9–20 is even more problematical. The inference that the twofold solution to the question of Marinus may have originated with Origen is also conjectural. But it is a conjecture that has been favoured by proponents both for and against the authenticity of Mk. 16: 9–20. The twofold solution is Origenic in any case, and that it originates with Origen seems not unlikely. If this ambidexterous or ambiguous solution is from Origen, it provides evidence for the existence of manuscripts ending with ἐφοβοῦντο γάρ in the third century in such quantities as conservatively to argue for a late second-century origin for this reading. However, against

---

[1] In addition to his many other services to the church, Origen was sometimes called in by bishops from other areas to 'trouble-shoot' in ecclesiastical disputes.

this conjectural second-century evidence for omitting Mk. 16: 9–20, there is positive evidence for its inclusion at this time. Celsus seems to have known Mark with the longer ending around 180.[1] Irenaeus certainly knew Mk. 16: 9–20 at this time. So also did Tatian around 170. Justin Martyr probably knew these verses around 150. In fact, *external evidence from the second century for Mk. 16: 9–20 is stronger than for most other parts of that Gospel.*

Unlike writers of the fourth and fifth centuries, and possibly the third, none of these second-century authors shows any consciousness of a divided state in the textual witness. This suggests an origin for the text tradition for omission sometime during the second half rather than the first half of the second century, and some place in the Mediterranean world not frequented by these writers. Caesarea, Alexandria and Carthage come immediately to mind, with Alexandria the most likely of the three.

At this point it will be helpful to summarize the evidence through the fifth century for the firmly grounded dual tradition regarding the last twelve verses of Mark.

5. SUMMARY OF WITNESSES FOR INCLUSION

(A) The witness of Justin Martyr (*Apol.* 1.45), though there is no specific mention of Mark, appears to reflect Mark's influence: ἐξελθόντες πανταχοῦ ἐκήρυξαν, cf. Mk. 16: 20, ἐξελθόντες ἐκήρυξαν πανταχοῦ.

(B) Celsus (*c.* 177–80) seems to have known this ending.[2]

---

[1] See n. 2 below.

[2] Origen in Book II of his treatise against Celsus quotes Celsus as follows: 'After his death he [allegedly] rose again and showed the marks of his punishment and how his hands had been pierced. But who saw this? A half-frantic woman, as you say [γυνὴ πάροιστρος ὡς φατέ], and perhaps some other one of those who were deluded by the same sorcery' (*Contra Celsum* 2. 55). This is a rather loose reference to the resurrection stories preserved in our Gospels. It can neither be applied to any one of them separately nor all of them together. Only in John does Jesus show his wounds. But this was done in the presence of the disciples (John 20: 20), not just some woman or even in addition to her another as well. John does however feature a woman as the one to whom Jesus first appeared after the resurrection – Mary Magdalene. And not until after she had reported to the disciples did he appear to them. In any case Origen understands Celsus

(C) Irenaeus, *adv. Haer.* 3. 10. 5 quotes Mk. 16: 19 as from the Gospel of Mark.

(D) A third-century passage, sometimes attributed to Hippolytus, includes an interpretation of Mk. 16: 18.[1]

(E) Vincentius (Bishop of Thibaris near Carthage), at the Seventh Council of Carthage, A.D. 256, apparently made

to be attacking the credibility of the witness of Mary Magdalene, for later he writes: 'he [Celsus] refers to the words of the gospel saying that he showed the marks of his punishment after he had risen from the dead and how his hands had been pierced. And he asks: "Who saw this?" And discrediting the narrative of Mary Magdalene, who is related to have seen him, he replies "a half-frantic woman, as you say".' There can be little doubt that Celsus meant to pillory the Gospel accounts by referring to Mary Magdalene as πάροιστρος. But what was the basis for such a charge and what did it mean? It certainly meant that she was a person whose testimony would leave something to be desired. But why? What grounds could there have been for questioning the credibility of Mary Magdalene? In Luke we are told that she was one 'out of whom seven demons had been driven' (Lk. 8: 1). The literal meaning of the term πάροιστρος in this context is best understood if one keeps in mind the condition of a person who has been stung into a frenzy of madness by real or imagined tormentors.

Origen asserts that there was no evidence for Celsus' charge 'in the scriptural account which was the source upon which he drew for his criticism' (*Contra Celsum* 2.60). Now while Luke identifies Mary Magdalene as a woman who had been possessed by demons and while he mentions that she and the other woman who had come with Jesus from Galilee were at the tomb after the stone had been rolled away and saw the man who informed them that Jesus had been raised, he makes no mention of any appearance of Jesus to either of them. And while John does record an appearance of the resurrected Jesus to Mary Magdalene, he makes no reference to her as a woman from whom demons had been cast out.

We could reason that it was John's account of Mary Magdalene weeping as she stood outside the tomb which prompted Celsus to disparage her condition for rendering reliable testimony. Or we could reason that Celsus read of the appearance of the resurrected Jesus to Mary Magdalene in John in the light of the statement about her in Lk. 8: 1. But by far the simplest solution to all this is to assume that Celsus was prompted by the account of the resurrection appearances in Mark to make his disparaging comment. For there it is recorded that Jesus, after his resurrection, 'appeared first to Mary Magdalene, from whom he had cast out seven demons'.

[1] Cf. B. S. Easton (ed. and trans.), *The Apostolic Tradition of Hippolytus* (Cambridge, 1934), pp. 60–1; Gregory Dix (ed. and trans.), *The Treatise on the Apostolic Tradition of St Hippolytus of Rome* (London, 1937), p. 58. Dix discusses the question of attribution on pp. 84–5. The third-century date and Roman provenance of the passage are not disputed.

reference to Mk. 16: 15–18 as authoritative along with its parallel, Matt. 28: 19.[1]

(F) Porphyry (c. 270) seems to have based an argument upon Mk. 16: 18 in Book VI of his work κατὰ χριστιανῶν.[2]

(G) *Acta Pilati* (Gospel of Nicodemus) contains Mk. 16: 15–18.[3]

(H) Eusebius knew copies of Mark containing verses 16: 9–20. This much is clear from the text published by Mai.

(I) Aphraates, earliest known Father of the Syrian church, cites Mk. 16: 16, 17 and 18 in a homily dated A.D. 337. Aphraates writes in Syriac and cites from a text of Mark to be distinguished from the Curetonian Syriac version as well as from the Peshitta. The importance of this is that it makes of this dated homily an additional quite independent witness to the ending of Mark in question coeval at least with B and ℵ.[4]

(J) Ambrose, Archbishop of Milan (d. 397), quotes from Mk. 16: 9–20 frequently.[5]

---

[1] Cf. *The Seventh Council of Carthage under Cyprian, ANF*, V, 569; *PL*, III, 1105. The citation in *PL* is identified with Matt. 10: 8 rather than with Mk. 16: 17–18. But examination of the text will bear out the editors of the *ANF* who prefer Mk. 16: 17–18 to Matt. 10: 8: 'Ite, in nomine meo manum imponite, daemonia expellite.'

[2] Cf. T. W. Crafer, 'The work of Porphyry against the Christians, and its reconstruction', 2 pts, *JTS*, 15 (1914), 504. We are indebted to *The Apocriticus of Macarius Magnes*, a work attributed to an Oriental bishop of that name who flourished at the beginning of the fifth century, for preserving what is attributed to Porphyry. Crafer argues that his Apology or Response was actually written by an anonymous Origenist of the fourth century and locates its provenance in Syria. He also conjectures that the actual wording of the pagan arguments against Christianity preserved in it originated with the Neoplatonic philosopher Hierocles, who as governor in Egypt persecuted the Christians at the beginning of the fourth century. In this case, Hierocles is believed to be dependent upon Porphyry for the content of his work. Crafer, 'The work of Porphyry', pp. 360ff. Cf. A. B. Hulen, *Porphyry's Work against the Christians: an Interpretation, YSR*, 1 (Scottdale, Pa., 1933), pp. 8–9.

[3] Cf. E. Hennecke, *New Testament Apocrypha* (2 vols., Philadelphia, 1963–5), I, 462; C. Tischendorf, *Evangelia Apocrypha* (Leipzig, 1853), pp. 243, 351.

[4] Cf. Burgon, *Last Twelve Verses*, pp. 26–7, for a discussion of the complex question of attribution.

[5] Mk. 16: 15: *On the Holy Spirit* 2. 145, *NPNF*[2], x, 133; *Of the Christian Faith* 1. 86, *NPNF*[2], x, 216. Mk. 16: 15–18: *On the Holy Spirit* 2. 151, *NPNF*[2], x, 134. Mk. 16: 17–18: *Concerning Repentance* 1. 35, *NPNF*[2], x, 335.

(K) Epiphanius of Constantia (Salamis) in *Panarion* [*Adversus Haereses*] (374–6) refers to Mk. 16: 19.[1]

(L) Chrysostom, Bishop of Constantinople (d. 407), makes an unmistakable reference to Mk. 16: 9.[2]

(M) *The Apostolic Constitutions*, written in Syria c. 380, contains in Book VI a quotation of Mk. 16: 15, and in Book VIII a quotation of Mk. 16: 17–18.[3]

(N) Jerome (d. 420) includes the verses in his Vulgate.

(O) Augustine (d. 430) discusses these verses as the work of Mark on numerous occasions.

(P) Nestorius in a sermon published in 429 quotes Mk. 16: 20, and Cyril of Alexandria the year following, writing against Nestorius, accepts this quotation.[4]

(Q) Mk. 16: 19 is cited in the second of the five Easter sermons in Gregory of Nyssa's *In sanctum Pascha sive in Christi resurrectionem*.[5]

We must add to these second- to fifth-century witnesses, Tatian's Diatessaron (second century), and the earliest versions – Itala, Syriac, Coptic, all of which attest the authenticity of these verses. It is clear that the acceptance of the last twelve verses of Mark was widespread. Throughout the ancient church, from Alexandria, Hippo, Carthage, Rome, Salamis, Constantinople, Antioch, Edessa, and Caesarea, the evidence for knowledge and acceptance of the authenticity of the last twelve verses of Mark in the ancient church is impressive.

We must also include the witness of the lectionary systems of the ancient church.

(A) The Synaxaria of the Greek church require Mk. 16: 9–20 to be read for Matins on Ascension Day.

(B) This same lection was adopted among the Syrians by the Melchite churches.[6]

---

[1] The reference can most conveniently be found in *PG*, XLI, 821. Cf. another but less clear reference to Mk. 16: 9, *PG*, XLI, 1057.

[2] *Homilies on First Corinthians*, *NPNF*[1], XII, 229.

[3] For bibliographical references, see J. Quasten, 'Apostolic constitutions', *The New Catholic Encyclopedia* (15 vols., New York, 1967), I, p. 690.

[4] *Adversus Nestorium* 2. 6, *PG*, LXXVI, 85 C.

[5] *PG*, XLVI, 651. M. A. Kugener attributes this sermon to Severus of Antioch (465–538), cf. J. Quasten, *Patrology* (3 vols., Westminster, Md., 1951–60), II, 277, who regards this attribution as proven.

[6] R. P. Smith, *Codices syriacos carshunicos, mendaeos, complectens*, Catalogi codicum manuscriptorum bibliothecae Bodleianae, pt 6 (Oxford, 1864), pp. 116, 127.

(C) According to the Evangelistarium used by the Jacobite Copts, Mk. 16: 14–20 was read at the liturgy on Ascension Day.[1]

(D) Mk. 16: 9–20 constituted the third of eleven lections which were read successively on Sundays at Matins throughout the year; as well as daily throughout Easter week in both Greek and Syrian churches.[2]

(E) Mk. 16: 9–20 was read at Matins for the second Sunday after Easter in both Greek and Syrian churches.[3]

(F) In the Monophysite churches of Syria, Mk. 16: 9–18 was read at Matins on Easter Tuesday.[4]

(G) Augustine writes that these same verses were read publicly during Easter among the churches in Africa. They are also included in the oldest lectionary of the Roman church.[5]

To the extent that this lectionary survey is complete and accurate, it seems clear that the last twelve verses of Mark occupied an important place in the lectionaries of the ancient church. They were read in the Greek and Syrian churches at least once every eleven weeks throughout the year, and were featured during two of the great festivals of the church – Easter and Ascension Day. According to Baumstark's Law the lections associated with the great festivals seem to have been the earliest to have been adopted.[6]

The present lectionary system seems to have originated and developed in the fourth century.[7] Once Mk. 16: 9–20 was stably set in the liturgy it would presumably have become increasingly difficult for copyists to omit these verses from their copies of Mark. This would have been a contributing factor to

---

[1] Paul A. de Lagarde, *Orientalia* (2 vols., Göttingen, 1879–80), I, 9. S. C. Malan (ed. and trans.), *Original Documents of the Coptic Church* (6 vols., London, 1872–5), IV, 63.

[2] Smith, *Codices syriacos*, p. 127.

[3] *Ibid.*, p. 116.   [4] *Ibid.*, p. 146.

[5] *Divi Hieronymi comes sive lectionarius*, in Jacobus Pamelius, *Liturgica Latinorum* (2 vols., Cologne, 1571), II, 27.

[6] Anton Baumstark, *Comparative Liturgy* (London, 1958), pp. 27ff. However, in the case of a feast of the Ascension distinct from Pentecost we seem to have no reliable testimony before Gregory of Nyssa's sermon on the Ascension delivered 18 May 388, Quasten, *Patrology*, II, 277.

[7] Allen Wikgren, 'Chicago studies in the Greek lectionary of the New Testament', *Biblical and Patristic Studies in Memory of Robert Pierce Casey*, eds. J. N. Birdsall and R. W. Thomson (Freiburg, 1963), pp. 120–1.

3-2

the eventual demise of the once popular practice of ending copies of Mark with ἐφοβοῦντο γάρ.

However, to account for the *adoption* of these verses in the lectionary system of the fourth century is another matter. This seems to require the admission that in the fourth century these verses were widely accepted as an authentic part of the text of Mark. This is important for it has been determined that lectionary readings 'serve as valuable supporting witnesses to readings found in the earliest, pre-recensional documents'.[1]

It would seem more likely that the last twelve verses of Mark were given the well-established place they have in the lectionaries of the ancient church at a time when they were *not* in question than at a time when they *were*. But this suggests, in the light of Mai's text and the scholium found at the end of Victor of Antioch's Commentary, that these verses had already entered some of the lectionaries of the ancient church by the time of Eusebius, and if Origen be made responsible for the basic substrata of Mai's text, by the beginning of the third century if not the end of the second. But to recognize this only serves to accentuate the problem created by the existence of a situation by the fifth century, possibly by the fourth or even by the third, where it could be said that the textual tradition ending Mark with ἐφοβοῦντο γάρ was strongly attested by contemporary manuscript evidence. How can we understand two so diametrically opposed and self-contradictory textual traditions developing in the church – and existing in at least some places, *side by side*? To do so we must note the Alexandrian influence upon the manuscript tradition.

6. B, ℵ, AND THE ARMENIAN VERSION: THE CHIEF WITNESSES FOR OMISSION

In the descriptions that follow I draw from the work of C. R. Williams who has fully set forth the witnesses for the text tradition ending Mark with ἐφοβοῦντο γάρ.[2]

---

[1] *Ibid.*, p. 121.

[2] C. R. Williams, 'The appendices to the Gospel according to Mark: a study in textual transmission', *Connecticut Academy of Arts and Sciences. Transactions*, 18 (New Haven, 1915), pp. 347–447.

We shall begin by a consideration of two famous fourth-century Greek uncials, B and ℵ, both of which end Mark with ἐφοβοῦντο γάρ.

(A) *The provenance of B and ℵ:* although these two uncials are at variance with one another at many points, when compared to all other ancient New Testament manuscripts they are seen to be closely related both as to provenance and text. Some of the considerations which have led scholars to adopt Egypt or even Alexandria as the place of origin for both B and ℵ are as follows:

(1) There is remarkable palaeographical evidence linking B and ℵ to Papyrus Rylands 28. The palaeographical peculiarities of these three manuscripts are such as to suggest that all three came from the same scriptorium. Since Papyrus Rylands 28 was found in Egypt, an Egyptian location seems likely for the scriptorium. Such palaeographical evidence is weakened, however, by the lack of papyri from outside Egypt.

(2) The orthographical evidence links B and ℵ with the spelling found in the papyri of Egypt.

(3) There is an extraordinary resemblance between the Psalms in the Coptic text of *Pistis Sophia* and the text of ℵ, which supports an Egyptian provenance for ℵ.

(4) No non-Alexandrian writer has been found who used the text peculiarly common to B and ℵ.

(5) The archetype of B contained the epistles in an order found elsewhere only in the Sahidic version. This would seem to have been an old Egyptian or Alexandrian order.

On the other hand there is evidence that at least ℵ was once in the library at Caesarea as is shown by a later hand responsible for a colophon at the end of Esther and also at the end of Ezra.

(B) *The text of B and ℵ:* the text peculiarly common to B and ℵ was used by most if not all Egyptian fathers after the end of the third century.

These seem to be the most important facts of the case. What are we to make of them? We have noticed that the two earliest and most important manuscript witnesses for the text tradition ending Mark with ἐφοβοῦντο γάρ can be traced to fourth-century Egypt – probably to Alexandria and possibly to the

37

same scriptorium in that city. Where do we turn next to find strong manuscript evidence supporting the omission of the last twelve verses of Mark? The strongest, least ambiguous and most consistent manuscript witness to a text tradition omitting Mk. 16: 9–20 outside the Egyptian witnesses is given by the Armenian version. The point is not merely that there are important Armenian manuscripts which end Mark with verse eight. The point is that a careful study of the Armenian version as a whole makes clear that it originally did not contain Mk. 16: 9–20. This means that in the fifth century in Armenia when this version was made the Gospel of Mark was believed to have ended with ἐφοβοῦντο γάρ. This is altogether consonant with the situation depicted in the text published by Mai, and in the statements associated with Victor of Antioch to the effect that there were in existence in the ancient church copies of Mark, indeed 'very many', which omitted 16: 9–20. But it is more, much more, than just consonant with this situation. It further illuminates the situation. It means that in the eyes of ecclesiastical authorities as well as scholars in Armenia the case for ending Mark with ἐφοβοῦντο γάρ was regarded as strong. That is, for these authorities the truth must have seemed to be the very opposite of what it seemed to be for the author of the scholium found in Victor of Antioch's commentary. How could this be? What opportunity did they have to come to a conclusion the exact opposite of that expressed in this scholium – and contrary to the 'Palestinian exemplar' referred to therein?

At this point it will be necessary to do two things to make certain we have firmly grasped the significance of the witness of the Armenian version. First – we must review the evidence indicating that the original Armenian version did not contain the last twelve verses of the Gospel of Mark. Second – we must survey the historical circumstances under which this version was produced and document that there was a close relationship between Alexandrian scholarship and the Armenian church, not only indirectly through Origen's continuing influence, but directly through Armenian scholars who in the early fifth century were specifically sent to Alexandria to study in order that they might bring back with them Alexandrian methods that could guide the Armenian authorities and further the vital task of producing a trustworthy version of the scriptures in the language of the Armenian people.

The evidence and arguments leading to the firm conclusion that the original Armenian version did not contain Mk. 16: 9–20 have been clearly set forth by E. C. Colwell.[1]

Not only do the majority of Armenian manuscripts omit Mk. 16: 9–20, but a significant proportion of those which include these verses present them in such a way as to indicate an earlier omission. In some codices these verses appear in a later hand. In others these verses are separated in some way from the rest of the Gospel. Many include the usual Armenian subscription after verse 8, etc. But what is more striking is the fact that when the Armenian manuscripts which can be dated before the thirteenth century are examined, those which omit Mk. 16: 9–20 predominate proportionately over those which include these verses, seven to one.

In addition to all this the increased textual variations in Mk. 16: 9–20 strongly suggest that these verses had a separate history from the comparatively unified manuscript tradition for the rest of the Armenian version.

Moreover a daughter version to the Armenian, i.e. the Old Georgian, appears to have been translated either directly from, or under the influence of, an Armenian prototype which omitted Mk. 16: 9–20. This is a strong indication that the authorized text of Mark in Armenian, when the Georgian translation was made in the late fifth century, omitted these verses. This is important in that it confirms that what obtains among the oldest extant Armenian manuscripts, which are from the ninth to the twelfth centuries, also obtained in the fifth. Finally, from a much later time, but indicative of an orthodox position, there is a commentary on Mark written by an archbishop Basilius, brother of the king, dated A.D. 1611, which comments on the text no farther than 16: 8.

Taken together these considerations very strongly indicate that the original Armenian version did not contain the last twelve verses of Mark. The importance of the outcome of this investigation emerges more clearly when we think geographically and chronologically about the contrast between the fifth-

---

[1] E. C. Colwell, 'Mark 16: 9–20. In the Armenian version', *JBL*, 56 (1937), 369–86.

century Armenian and Georgian versions and the earlier versions from the second and third centuries, i.e. Old Latin, Syriac, and Coptic (Sahidic).

7. ALEXANDRIA AND THE CHIEF WITNESSES FOR OMISSION

The balance of evidence in the case of the Old Latin, Syriac and Coptic versions weighs in favour of the inclusion of Mk. 16: 9–20 in the Greek prototype on which they were based. That is to say, not only on both its flanks, in Africa and in Syria, but within Egypt itself, the earlier versions in the vernacular, on balance, tell against the fourth-century Alexandrian witness of B and ℵ and against the witness of the fifth-century Armenian and Georgian versions.

The witness of the earlier versions in favour of including Mk. 16: 9–20 is explicitly supported by the witness of such second-century Fathers of the church as Justin, Tatian and Irenaeus. This combined versional and patristic testimony as well as the testimony of the lectionaries naturally suggests the conclusion that the omission of the last twelve verses of Mark in the original Armenian and the dependent Old Georgian versions may be related to the omission of these same verses in a particular textual tradition having its origin in Alexandria, and represented in B and ℵ.

In the fourth century, Armenian Christians had contact with Alexandrian traditions primarily through Cappadocian Christianity. Students and admirers of Origen had held some of the very highest positions of trust in the Cappadocian churches.[1] Therefore, Cappadocian scholars and church leaders were no strangers to Alexandrian textual scholarship.[2]

---

[1] Origen himself was for a relatively short time in Caesarea of Cappadocia. Cf. Eusebius, *Ecc. Hist.* 6. 27.

[2] The appeal of Alexandrian learning was very broad and inclusive. The respect for Alexandrian textual scholarship should be seen in the context of a general overall high regard for the achievements of Alexandrian research. H. I. Marrou, *A History of Education in Antiquity* (New York, 1956), p. 190, in reference to the role of the museum in Alexandria in the higher scientific education of antiquity, writes: 'In the fourth century Alexandria was a great university city, particularly famous for medicine, and it

Gregory the Illuminator, under whose leadership the whole Armenian nation became Christian, was educated in Caesarea of Cappadocia. Later the king of Armenia sent Gregory back to this same city to be consecrated bishop of the Armenian church.

Through Gregory the total and official conversion of Armenia was achieved. He became the most highly venerated figure in Armenian history. It was not just Gregory that was held in honour, but his descendants were similarly revered. What was done by Gregory, including receiving his education in Caesarea of Cappadocia, became a custom which was followed more or less regularly by many of his successors. Thus the relationship with Cappadocia was maintained for many years after his death.[1]

The question of the textual history of the Armenian version is complicated by the extremely complex and unsettled state of the question concerning the Caesarean text. The essentials of the matter seem to be as follows:

(A) The works of Robert Blake on the old Georgian version and Stanislas Lyonnet on the Armenian version show that these versions are akin to a particular text type which can be identified with the text common to Θ, 700, and 565; a text that can also be discerned in some of the New Testament citations of Origen and Eusebius.[2]

(B) This particular text type may never have existed as a definite recension which then served as the parent of all the related progeny. For there are indications that it may have been

attracted students from far and wide – from as far away as Cappadocia, as we know from the case of Caesarius, the brother of St Gregory [of] Nazianzen: the best way for a doctor to impress his patients was to let them know that he had studied at Alexandria.' This provides some idea of the great initial advantage that Origen had wherever he went. As a scholar who had studied in Alexandria, indeed was himself a native son of the place, he enjoyed the prestige that always accompanies being associated with a great centre of learning.

[1] Cf. Karekin Sarkissian, *The Council of Chalcedon and the Armenian Church* (London, 1965), pp. 76ff.

[2] Cf. E. C. Colwell, 'The significance of grouping of New Testament manuscripts', *NTS*, 4 (1958), 78–9; Bruce M. Metzger, 'The Caesarean text of the Gospels', *JBL*, 64 (1945), 457–89; S. Lyonnet, 'La première version arménienne des Evangiles', *RB*, 47 (1938), 355–82; R. P. Blake, Kirsopp Lake and Silva New, 'The Caesarean text of the Gospel of Mark', *HTR*, 21 (1928), 286–307.

the result of a process whereby texts were produced in the light of a critical comparison of existing manuscripts representing divergent textual tendencies.

We are encouraged to imagine that widely travelled scholars like Origen, faced by divergent text traditions in the third-century church, not satisfied with adhering always to even the best local text, would at times quite consciously produce for their own use, as well as the use of their students, 'critical' texts of books or parts of books as the changing situation might require. Since the number of authoritative text traditions laying claim upon an exegete like Origen was limited to the best from his native place and those most highly regarded in other places, the results of these third-century 'critical' efforts were in general predictable. They would exhibit little in common that could not be found in one of the existing second-century text types, and since these 'critical' texts were being produced on an eclectic basis without the controlling influence from an authorized scholar or group of scholars commissioned to produce a new recension according to uniform and agreed-upon principles, it would never be possible to reconstruct a *Vorlage* of this 'Caesarean' text. In general such an understanding of the matter will go a long way in explaining the mystery of the 'Caesarean text'.[1]

(C) On the other hand, if there ever was a second-century text type from which the 'Caesarean' text type is descended, it probably was Egyptian in provenance and is to be seen in such Egyptian representatives as: W^{mk}, P37, Berlin P13416, and P45. It would appear on these terms that Origen made use of manuscripts exhibiting this text tradition, but generally, or often, corrected them by other manuscripts representing other text types. Indeed on these terms it would appear that he actually popularized his version of this text type during the twenty-five years he carried on exegetical work in Caesarea, thus accounting for the widespread distribution of this text type outside Egypt and associating it to this extent with Caesarea.

(D) That Origen first encountered this text type in Caesarea

---

[1] I am conscious of the fact that at this point I have gone beyond any explicit statement made by experts on the 'Caesarean' text. But having read what they have written, it seems to me that this view of the matter is the one that is implicit in what they have discovered about this text, and that it does more justice to the apparent facts of the case than any other known to me.

(so Streeter) seems to have been disproved by the discovery of Kirsopp Lake and his colleagues that Origen cited a text of Mark as it is represented in the 'Caesarean' text type while he was in Alexandria and before his migration to Caesarea. Of course Origen had been in Caesarea previously and manuscripts from Caesarea in any case could have been found in Alexandria. But Lake's discovery does destroy the basis for Streeter's argument that this text type should be called 'Caesarean', for Streeter argued that before Origen left Alexandria to reside in Caesarea he used an Alexandrian text – presumably, according to Streeter, the authoritative text in that locality.[1]

(E) Lake observed, contrary to Streeter, that Origen used a B $\aleph$ text in his citations from Mark in Books VI–X of his Commentary on John, which books, according to Eusebius, were written while Origen was in Caesarea.[2] This means that Origen continued to use a B $\aleph$ text of Mark after he left Alexandria. Lake, agreeing with Griesbach, finds that there was a change in Origen's text of Mark, which change came in the middle of chapter 12. Before that point the text rather consistently agreed with B $\aleph$ C L Δ. But after that point 'it sometimes agrees with this group and sometimes with various "Western" authorities, and in this oscillation it agrees with family Θ'. Lake then goes on to observe that in his Commentary on Matthew, written later, Origen did not use a text for his quotations from Mark which was closely akin to B $\aleph$, but rather followed a text agreeing with family Θ throughout the whole of Mark. Lake then concluded, 'So far as we can see, this text was the text which he used for the rest of his life.'[3]

(F) The Greek manuscripts of family Θ witness for the inclusion of Mk. 16: 9–20. Streeter's inference that these verses were originally absent from family Θ is unwarranted. They are not only present in Θ, but in both 565[mk] and 700. The scholia Streeter noted on 1, 22 and 1582 witness to the existence of a manuscript tradition favouring omission. But the inclusion of Mk. 16: 9–20 in all these manuscripts indicates that the tradition for inclusion was stronger. Streeter's main witness for omission in family Θ came from the Armenian version.[4]

---

[1] Blake et al., 'Caesarean text', pp. 259–77; Streeter, Four Gospels, pp. 91–101.
[2] Ecc. Hist. 6. 24.   [3] Blake et al., 'Caesarean text', pp. 259–77.
[4] Streeter, Four Gospels, p. 88.

What does all this mean for our understanding of the history of the Armenian version? We may suggest the following implications:

(A) Origen himself, for the greater part of the twenty-five-year period he was in Caesarea of Palestine, was not a champion of the B ℵ text, certainly not to the exclusion of other text types.

(B) Origen knew and respected manuscripts related to the B ℵ text type. These possibly, perhaps likely, omitted Mk. 16: 9–20. Origen therefore, on principle, according to his own mode of operation, would not only for himself have insisted on an openness to the possibility that these verses were secondary to the original text of Mark, but he would have expected his students to maintain a similar openness.

(C) Origen's use of a different text type agreeing with family Θ does not represent a rejection of the B ℵ text type. For at many points the newly adopted text type was inclusive of readings otherwise found only in the B ℵ text type tradition.

(D) Therefore, any influence of Origen upon the Armenian version through his well-known influence upon Cappadocian scholars, both from contacts made in Caesarea of Palestine and during his stay in Cappadocia, would not likely have been decisively either for or against omission of Mk. 16: 9–20, but rather for an 'openness' on the question.

(E) Such a school heritage of 'openness' could have helped prepare the way for, and could have facilitated the adoption of, an 'Alexandrian' witness for omission brought back by Armenian scholars who were sent to study in Egypt in the fifth century.

This development assumes that the practice of ending Mark with ἐφοβοῦντο γάρ which we see evident in B ℵ was by the fifth century strongly championed in some Alexandrian textual circles and sufficiently prevalent in some parts of the church outside Armenia, that the Armenian authorities could risk repercussions from conservatives within the church by omitting these verses. However, for reasons that will be brought out below, it was precisely in such a highly centralized and established national church where the very life of the people was constituted by the scriptures, that certain serious objections to teaching contained in these verses could have led the authorities to cast the weight of their influence into the balance on the side of omission, especially if it seemed to scholars to be a question on which there was strong support for either omission or inclusion.

At the beginning of the fifth century the project of producing an official Armenian version of the scriptures was undertaken under the overall supervision of the patriarch catholicos Sahak, a descendant of Gregory the Illuminator. This project was first undertaken at a time when the Armenian king wanted to strengthen his ties with Byzantium, and if possible to reunite his kingdom (at this time a part of the Persian Empire) to that part of Armenia which had previously been ceded to the Romans in an earlier partition plan enforced by the great powers. The Persians were displeased over this move toward reunification, and the Armenian king, in reality a client prince of the Persians, was deposed. The patriarch Sahak, however, was successful in reassuring the Persians that he had no such political intentions and was able to continue with his plans for producing a single authorized version of the scriptures for the entire Armenian nation.

Up until this time the Armenian church had been liturgically trilingual. The scriptures were read in Syriac in those churches which long before had been evangelized from Syria to the south, but they were read in Greek in those which came into being in response to the missionary activity of Gregory the Illuminator. In either case the explanation of the scriptures was given in the vernacular.

Given these circumstances it is possible to view the peculiar character of the Armenian version as it has been delineated by text critics as a comprehensible expression of the realities of the political, social and ecclesiastical forces affecting the Armenian nation at that time.

The action of Sahak was circumspect and imaginative. He took precautions to see that his scholars would be adequately prepared for their task and free from undue pressure from any quarter. It was necessary that the translation be acceptable to all major parties. Special precautions had to be taken to satisfy churches traditionally tied to Syrian Christianity, since discontent in that quarter could be exploited by the Syrophile elements who realized the peril of strengthening ecclesiastical contacts with Byzantium; contacts sought by Sahak in reviving a policy of his glorious predecessor Gregory the Illuminator, and reversing a policy which after partition had virtually prevented contact with Caesarea in Cappadocia and Constantinople. Christianity in Persia had come from Syria and the Iranophile elements in Armenia realized that maintaining close and harmonious relationships with the Syrian churches was a national asset as long as most of Armenia was under Persian hegemony.

For all these reasons, as well as for sound scholarly considerations, Sahak appropriated large sums to support scholars. Some were sent to Edessa, to study and prepare themselves to handle the Syriac documents responsibly. Yet for all his efforts in this direction, Sahak, the last descendant of Gregory the Illuminator's family, was a Hellenophile in his heart and mind.[1] His father, Nerses the Great, like Gregory before him, had been educated in Caesarea of Cappadocia, and had encouraged and strengthened the Hellenophile influence in Armenia. Sahak himself was actually born in Caesarea of Cappadocia, and probably was sent back by his father to that city for some of his advanced studies. His mastery of the Greek language and literature helped him in his leadership of Armenian intellectual life in the fifth century, centred as it was on a translation movement of which the translation of the scriptures was only a part. Scholars were also dispatched to various Greek cities, including Constantinople and Alexandria, but Cappadocia continued to provide an important avenue of influence upon Armenian scholarship.

The result of Sahak's efforts to prepare his scholars by providing for their travel and study was the production of a version of the New Testament which cannot but command the respect of modern text critics. It was produced by scholars who were linguistically well trained and who were in the enviable position of knowing at first hand the manuscript traditions of a large part of fifth-century Christendom. Thus, under the circumstances, it is perfectly natural that this version should show kinship with the Syriac version and with all the major fourth-century text types known to modern scholars.

---

[1] 'This family was still held in the highest veneration by the Armenian people as a natural expression of their gratitude to St Gregory the Illuminator for his great work of converting Armenia to Christianity.' Sarkissian, *Council of Chalcedon*, p. 100.

The following church Fathers make no reference to Mk. 16: 9–20: Tertullian of Carthage (d. after 220); Cyprian, Bishop of Carthage (d. 258); Athanasius, Bishop of Alexandria (d. 373); Basil, Bishop of Caesarea in Cappadocia (d. *c.* 379); Cyril of Jerusalem (d. 386); Gregory of Nazianzus in Cappadocia (d. 389 or 390); Gregory of Nyssa in Cappadocia (d. 394); Cyril of Alexandria (d. 444). Other names could be added but these stand out as Fathers who clearly had the opportunity to cite these verses and in some cases could have found support for their views by appealing to some of these verses. Their silence, therefore, seems significant. It seems noteworthy that after the third century, it is the Alexandrian and Cappadocian Fathers who dominate this list.

8. REMAINING MANUSCRIPT WITNESSES FOR OMISSION

In addition to B and ℵ, Williams lists three other uncials which support an original ending for Mark at ἐφοβοῦντο γάρ: L, 7¹² and Ψ. All three have verses 9–20. These verses, however, are separated from v. 8 (e.g. by another ending as well as in other ways) and it is clear that they are secondary to Mk. 1: 1 – 16: 8 in the text tradition of these particular manuscripts.

The essential information regarding each is as follows:

(1) L, Egyptian provenance; date, eighth century; text related especially to B and the text represented in the citations of Origen.

(2) 7¹² (0112), Egyptian provenance; date, seventh century; text related to B and L.

(3) Ψ, Egyptian provenance; date, eighth or ninth century; text mixed.

(4) Williams also discusses fragment T¹ (099), Egyptian in provenance, dated seventh or eighth century, about the text of which he writes: 'Since the fragment consists of one folio it is not possible to determine accurately the text relations, but since the other uncials showing the double ending are allied to ℵ B it seems probable that this MS is related to the same family.'[1]

(5) Williams also discusses a cursive that clearly witnesses

---

[1] Williams, 'The appendices', p. 416.

against the authenticity of Mk. 16: 9–20, cursive 579; provenance uncertain; date, eighth century; text related to B and א. Williams conjectures that it was descended from an uncial of the L type.

(6) The seventh-century cursive 2386, which witnesses for omission, is not discussed by Williams.[1]

The conclusion to be drawn from this survey of the Greek manuscripts is that support for an earlier form of Mark ending with ἐφοβοῦντο γάρ appears to be traceable to manuscripts originating in Egypt and generally related to the B א type text.

The witness from the Old Latin version is the same as that from the Greek texts. The single Old Latin codex witnessing for omission is Codex Bobiensis (k), a fifth-century manuscript, originating in North Africa, and exhibiting a text containing many scribal blunders, suggesting that the writer was a Greek scribe with very little knowledge of Latin. Tischendorf conjectured that he was an Alexandrian calligraph wholly ignorant of Latin. The text type as to family affiliation is mixed and perplexing, but it includes 'considerable affinity with the early Alexandrian text as represented by א B and agrees with it in omitting the longer conclusion'.[2] Codex Bobiensis does not end Mark with 16: 8, but concludes with the famous shorter ending for Mark for which Williams succeeds in demonstrating an Egyptian origin. It is this same Egyptian shorter ending that is included between verses 8 and 9 in L, ד¹², Ψ, 099 and 579 discussed above. However, in all these seventh- to eighth-century manuscripts, unlike the fifth-century Bobiensis, this shorter Egyptian ending is followed by Mk. 16: 9–20, clearly indicating, as Williams correctly concludes, that the double-ending textual tradition is a later development than the scribal practice of including only the shorter ending. Williams points out that this later double-ending textual tradition is found in an eleventh-century Sahidic and also a late Bohairic manuscript. It is also found in some late Ethiopian manuscripts.

An eighth- or ninth-century Arabic manuscript, Rom. Vat.

---

[1] Bruce Metzger in *A Textual Commentary on the Greek New Testament* (London, New York, 1971), p. 122, following Kurt Aland, questions whether 2386 is a true witness for omission. Metzger lists the additional twelfth-century Greek manuscript 304 as a witness for omission.

[2] Williams, 'The appendices', p. 403.

Arab. 13, was listed by Tischendorf and Tregelles as a witness for omission and is sometimes so listed today. However, Abbé Martin, in his *Introduction to New Testament Criticism*, had already reported an opposite conclusion after a careful examination of the manuscript by the time Williams wrote, and Williams rightly concluded: 'We find, therefore, that Arabic 13 is in reality of no significance in discussing this question, but it has been examined lest we seem to overlook some of the testimony.'[1]

The only important manuscript witnessing for the omission of Mk. 16: 9–20 that remains to be considered is the now famous Sinaitic Syriac (S^s) found by Mrs Agnes Smith Lewis in 1892 in St Catherine's Monastery in Sinai, where, years before, Tischendorf made his famous discovery of Codex Sinaiticus א which has loomed so large in our discussions up until this point.

Although associated with א both by its place of discovery and by its designation in modern scholarship, its original provenance appears to have been Syria, and its text seems to afford no indication of a special relationship to B and א. The only significant relationship S^s has with B and א is in the omission of Mk. 16: 9–20. But, as has been noted above, at exactly this point it stands alone among the Syrian witnesses, contradicted by all other Syriac authorities: Tatian (second century); Peshitta (fourth to fifth century); Palestinian Syriac (fifth century); and Harclean Syriac (A.D. 616).

Our examination of the manuscript evidence indicates that S^s is an important exception to a general twofold rule: (1) the majority of manuscripts that can be dated before the tenth century favour the inclusion of Mk. 16: 9–20 (this includes such witnesses as A (fifth century), C (fifth century), D (sixth century), K (ninth century), W (fifth century), X (tenth century), Δ (ninth century), Θ (ninth century), Π (ninth century), family 13, 33 (ninth century), 565^{mk} (ninth century), 892 (ninth century), Itala aur (seventh century), c (twelfth to thirteenth century), d (fifth century), ff^2 (fifth century), l (seventh to eighth century), n (fifth century), o (seventh century), g (ninth century)); (2) manuscripts which witness for omission of Mk. 16: 9–20 are related to an Egyptian or Alexandrian text tradition, one respected in the scriptorium tradition governing the formation of B and א.

[1] *Ibid.*, p. 399.

9. EVALUATION OF THE MANUSCRIPT EVIDENCE

New Testament manuscripts can be grouped in families in terms of their textual similarities or kinship to one another. When we join this with the idea that some of these groups are like large families which share certain distinctive characteristics and that these groups have family ties to particular geographical regions, we have the basis for a theory of local texts. B. H. Streeter developed the idea of local texts and classified manuscripts accordingly to a fivefold scheme. Streeter's theory is not universally accepted, but it is one that is sufficiently respected, so that an analysis of the textual witnesses for and against Mk. 16: 9–20 according to this classification is worth making.

Under the five headings: (1) Alexandria, (2) Antioch, (3) Caesarea, (4) Italy and Gaul, and (5) Carthage, Streeter, in a descending order of importance, listed first his primary authority for each local text, then his secondary and tertiary authorities, followed by what he termed supplementary and patristic witness.

According to this classification the primary authority for the local text of Alexandria (B) witnesses for omission. However, the secondary, tertiary and supplementary witnesses are about evenly divided. The patristic witnesses are silent.

The primary authority for the local text of Antioch (Syr^s) witnesses for omission. However, the secondary, tertiary and supplementary witnesses are unanimous in support of including Mk. 16: 9–20.[1]

Streeter lists two primary authorities for the local text of Caesarea (Θ and 565^{mk}), and both witness for inclusion. The other authorities are divided, with the testimony of the Greek manuscripts favouring inclusion and the versional testimony of the Old Georgian and Old Armenian favouring omission. The patristic witness (Origen and Eusebius) is difficult to assess.

The primary authority for the local text of Italy and Gaul (D) witnesses for inclusion, as do all the secondary, tertiary, supplementary and patristic witnesses.

The primary authority for Carthage (k$^{mk\ mt}$) witnesses for omission. However, the other authorities witness for inclusion with the patristic witness being silent.

---

[1] Streeter lists no patristic witnesses for the local text of Antioch.

It is difficult to argue from these considerations to any conclusion, because there is a tendency, especially in Caesarean witnesses, for all texts to be accommodated to the Textus Receptus. Allowing for this, however, we may tentatively conclude that, based on Streeter's classification, the witness for omission is strong but not unanimous in the local text of Alexandria. The witness of the local text of Antioch is divided, but in balance seems to favour inclusion, unless the single witness of the primary authority is taken to outweigh the combined testimony of secondary, tertiary and supplementary authorities. The witness of the local text of Caesarea is also divided, but in balance favours inclusion, unless the authority of the versions outweighs the reading of the majority of Greek manuscript authorities, including both primary authorities. The witness for inclusion is strongest in the local text for Italy and Gaul – being unanimous at all levels of authority, including the patristic witnesses. The witness of the local text in Carthage is divided, with the primary (certainly) and patristic (possibly) favouring omission, but with the secondary and tertiary authorities favouring inclusion.

If this distribution be posted on a geographical map of the ancient Mediterranean world it will be seen to sustain Streeter's observation about the influence of propinquity. The witness for inclusion is unanimous in Italy and Gaul. It is strong but not unanimous in Syria. It is less strong still in Palestine. It is weakest in Egypt. In the region between Egypt and Italy, i.e. North Africa, the testimony for inclusion is not as weak as in Egypt but nowhere near as strong as in Italy and Gaul. The only exception to this pattern of 'kinship by virtue of geographical proximity' is the witness of the Armenian and Georgian versions. The kinship between these two versions is explained by propinquity, but their kinship with the local text of Alexandria with respect to the omission of Mk. 16: 9–20 invites an explanation which can account for some kind of 'geographical leap'.[1]

The distribution pattern of this textual variant can be described in reverse by saying that the witness for omission is strongest in Egyptian texts, that it is represented significantly in the authorities testifying to the character of the local texts in the

---

[1] See above, pp. 40ff. and below, pp. 71ff.

adjoining regions of Palestine and North Africa, that it is less strong in Syria and not found at all among Streeter's authorities for the local text in Italy and Gaul.

If each of these local texts be given an equal voice, we would have Alexandria favouring omission, Italy and Gaul favouring inclusion, with the other three affording a divided witness. Carthage seems to side with neighbouring Alexandria, but Antioch and Caesarea in balance seem to side with Italy and Gaul.

According to this analysis the textual evidence in balance seems to favour inclusion. However, if we were to concentrate attention upon Streeter's primary authorities alone the local texts of 'Caesarea' and 'Italy and Gaul' would be outvoted by the threefold agreement between Alexandria, Antioch and Carthage.

If the refinements of Streeter's local text theory be set aside and attention given to the witness of the three commonly recognized major textual groups, (1) Alexandrian, (2) Eastern (Caesarea and Antioch), and (3) Western (Italy–Gaul and North Africa), the witness of the Alexandrian manuscripts is predominantly for omission, the witness of the Western manuscripts is predominantly for inclusion, and the witness of the Eastern manuscripts is divided though in balance it favours inclusion.

A fourth group of manuscripts, that representing the readings of the later Byzantine recension, is virtually unanimous in favour of inclusion. However, since Westcott and Hort, the Byzantine type of text has been widely regarded as a later and more developed form of text, and its witness in this matter, therefore, is often not accorded much weight. This procedure is not beyond being challenged. For example, the fifth-century Codex A, which in most of the New Testament is a constant ally of B ℵ and representative of the Alexandrian type of text, in the Gospels is an example of the Byzantine type of text. Presumably the scribe of A copied the Gospels from a different exemplar than that which he employed for his text of the rest of the New Testament. The text of this exemplar of the Gospels was close to that created by Lucian in the fourth century. According to Streeter Lucian seems to have taken the Alexandrian (B ℵ) text as the basis for a revision representing the combined traditions of the great churches.[1] Except for the Alexandrian text, Lucian is believed to have had manuscripts of a greater variety and better quality than any we possess. And even for the Alexandrian text the manuscripts available to him would presumably have been of as good a quality as B and ℵ. Therefore, Lucian's decision to include Mk. 16: 9–20 in his recension must either be taken as that of a witness to the traditions of the great churches in the fourth century, or, in case he gave an uncritical priority to the text tradition of the church where he carried out his work (Antioch), it must be taken as a further witness that the local text of Antioch testifies for inclusion. However, it should be remembered that the Lucianic text is inclusive in principle. So it is possible even if somewhat unlikely that Lucian could have included the disputed verses had they been absent from most of his authorities.

E. C. Colwell has developed a view of the origin of text types which affords us still another way by which to evaluate the manuscript evidence.

(1) 'The Beta texttype [which we have referred to as B ℵ] is a "made" text probably Alexandrian in origin, produced in part by the selection of relatively "good old MSS" but more importantly by the philological editorial know-how of Alexandrians.'[2]

Colwell cites Günther Zuntz with approval when Zuntz writes: 'In the latter half of the second century the Alexandrian bishopric possessed a scriptorium, which by its output set the standard for the Alexandrian type of Biblical manuscript.'[3]

Assuming the existence of some such ecclesiastically sponsored scriptorial activity it is our suggestion that the practice of omitting the last twelve verses of Mark from at least some copies of Mark can with probability be traced back at least thus far in time and space. Certainly the omission of these verses from B and ℵ as well as the circumstances under which they have been included in Ψ, combined with the very close agreement between P75 and B, offers considerable support for such a conjecture,

---

[1] Streeter, *Four Gospels*, pp. 116ff.

[2] 'The origin of texttypes of New Testament manuscripts', *Early Christian Origins: Studies in Honor of Harold R. Willoughby*, ed. Allen Paul Wikgren (Chicago, 1961), p. 137.

[3] *Ibid.*, p. 131, quoting Günther Zuntz, *The Text of the Epistles* (Oxford, 1953), pp. 271–3.

i.e. that this reading was known in Alexandria by the end of the second century.

(2) 'The so-called Caesarean text type is not Caesarean and is at least two types, the earlier of which is a prototype, an early stage in the process which produced the mature Beta and Delta text types.'[1]

(3) 'The so-called Western text or Delta text type is the un-controlled popular text of the second century. It has no unity and should not be referred to as the "Western text".'[2]

In order to comprehend the significance for our problem of what Colwell has discovered about the probable development of the major text types we are invited to imagine the following: in the beginning there was an autograph of Mark, which was copied. Changes were introduced into the texts of successive copies of Mark. In this way as these copies were spread through-out the Mediterranean world the process of textual transmission involved a natural perpetuation of, and addition to, the changes introduced into the first copies. Thus developed a situation in the second century where there were copies of Mark existing throughout the church which contained many differences from the autograph, and which copies also differed considerably among themselves. Even at this time, however, there would have been familial kinships between manuscripts copied in particular scriptoria, and of course all copies would have been lineal descendants of the autograph. Some copies would probably have had mixed texts, as copyists sometimes shifted from one model to another in the process of making new copies. The process of checking this freewheeling and natural proliferation of textual changes probably began in different places at different times and for different reasons. And it may well have fluctuated in any one locality over a long period of time in accordance with the temper of the times and the temperature of ecclesiastical concern over the manuscript differences. It is unlikely that efforts to control the 'uncontrolled popular text of the second century' were limited to Alexandria. It is probable that wherever the monarchical bishopric developed, there, sooner or later, some effort to exert ecclesiastical influence, if not control, over the local preparation of biblical manuscripts was exercised. In addition to Alexandria, Antioch

---

[1] *Ibid.*, p. 138.   [2] *Ibid.*, p. 137.

was a most likely centre for the development of another standard for a type of biblical manuscript. We know the name of one of the later editors who made his contribution to the development of this Antiochean, or Syrian or Alpha text type. His name was Lucian and we know that his revised edition of this Antiochean text type was in principle inclusive. We know the name of another great biblical scholar, who, though he did not make an edition of the Greek New Testament, did exert some influence on the history of the New Testament text. His name was Origen. But for every name we know, there were many we do not know, who made their contributions during the third and fourth centuries to the process of controlling the proliferation of changes that earlier had been introduced into copies of the New Testament. Therefore, when we speak of the 'uncontrolled popular text of the second century' we must not think of a proto-'text type'. It was simply the state of the texts before concerted efforts were begun to bring the relatively uncontrolled process of textual change under control. And when we speak of the Delta text type as representative of this second-century text, we do not mean that manuscripts witnessing to this text type like D have descended from second-century progenitors along a line of copying where there has been no concerted effort to control the natural proliferation of textual change. We simply mean that these manuscripts seem to be *relatively* uninfluenced by the particular or peculiar efforts to 'make' a text which we can identify in the history of the Beta text type, on the one hand, or the Alpha text type, on the other. For example, any second-century manuscript of Mark which found its way to Lyons, and was copied there throughout the third and fourth centuries, would leave a progeny of manuscripts relatively free from the influence of the peculiar characteristics of textual controls originating in the 'philological know-how of the Alexandrians', as well as free from those tendencies characteristic of, or peculiar to, the 'text-making' process in Syria. The Delta text type, therefore, is simply a textual category inclusive of important manuscripts which, however closely related they may be to the other text types, are distinguishable from manuscripts belonging to these other text types by virtue of their giving one another significant support against the common readings of these other manuscripts. The range of agreement between these manuscripts is decisively lower than the range of agreement between manuscripts representing the Alpha and Beta text types, and this leads Colwell to question whether or not there is a Delta text type. Similarly, the range of agreement between manuscripts belonging to the so-called Gamma (Caesarean) text type is such that here again there is a question whether this is a text type!

In fact 565 turns out to be closer to the main representatives of the Alpha text type than it does to Θ. Yet Θ and 565 have always been regarded as two of the main Greek manuscript witnesses for the Caesarean text![1]

It is not easy to assay with precision the significance of Colwell's discoveries for our evaluation of the manuscript evidence bearing on the question of the authenticity of Mk. 16: 9–20. We have seen that the Beta text type witnesses for omission. We have good reason to presume that this text type was made under circumstances where 'relatively good old MSS' were selected as models for copying. The presumption might be that some and perhaps all of these omitted Mk. 16: 9–20.

The Alpha text type, on the other hand, witnesses for inclusion. And some readings of the Alpha text type have been verified as being early readings by papyrus finds in Egypt. With reference to P66 Colwell writes: 'Strangely enough to our previous ideas, the contemporary corrections in that papyrus frequently change an Alpha-type reading to a Beta-type reading (Hort's "Neutral"). This indicates that at this early period readings of both kinds were known, and the Beta-type were supplanting the Alpha-type – at least as far as this witness is concerned.'[2] Perhaps it would be more accurate to say that Beta-

---

[1] E. C. Colwell and Ernest W. Tune, 'The quantitative relationships between MS text-types', *Biblical and Patristic Studies in Memory of Robert Pierce Casey* (Freiburg, 1963), pp. 28–9.

[2] Colwell, 'Origin of texttypes', pp. 130–1. The significance of the support for Byzantine readings given by the papyri is fully developed by Harry A. Sturz, 'The use of the Byzantine text-type in New Testament textual criticism' (unpublished manuscript, 1967). Sturz, without claiming to be exhaustive, lists over 150 readings where N.T. papyri support distinctive readings of the Byzantine text. He also lists over 150 readings where N.T. papyri support readings found in the Byzantine text and in one or more witnesses to the Western text, but rejected by Westcott and Hort, i.e. where the papyri support a Byzantine–Western alignment against a reading found

type readings were supplanting the Alpha-type readings *in Egypt* – at least as far as this witness is concerned. In any case, the witness of A and the Alpha text type is for inclusion of Mk. 16: 9–20, and this reading, like other characteristics of the Alpha text type as over against the Beta text type, as the papyri show, may be early. In fact, because of patristic evidence, we *know* that this reading was early, certainly as early as the second century.

Fortunately, an appeal to the major Greek manuscripts not belonging to the Beta and Alpha text types presents a less divided picture. None witness for omission. On the other hand, and by way of contrast, the following important uncials witness for inclusion: D, W^mk, Θ. Broadly speaking, an agreement among these *relatively* independent witnesses gives us a reliable indication of an early pre-recensional reading. That is, such an agreement probably carries us back at least into the second century.

On balance, then, considering Colwell's views on the development of text types, we obtain the same general result. We find that early Greek manuscript evidence like the evidence of the early versions, on balance, witnesses for inclusion.[1]

Certainly by the fourth century there is clear evidence that the Beta text type ended Mark with ἐφοβοῦντο γάρ. However, as is clear from B (where the copyist has left a full column and

in the B ℵ text type and preferred by Westcott and Hort. In another list he gives 170 readings where Westcott and Hort followed a Byzantine–B ℵ alignment and where the papyri have subsequently confirmed these readings over against competing textual readings. From this evidence, as well as from other cogent considerations, Sturz concludes that the B ℵ text types, Western authorities *and* the Byzantine text, all should be regarded as potentially capable of preserving second-century readings. All three are capable of bearing independent witness to the state of the text in the second century.

[1] With Syr^s and k^mt mk as witnesses for omission, the strong witness for omission in the late Armenian and Georgian versions appears to have significant support from the earlier Syrian and Latin versions. This appearance of widespread geographical support in the versions for omission, when united with the witness for omission in B and ℵ, creates an impression of strong support for omission over all. However, such an impression is weakened when, upon investigation and reflection, one considers that, *on balance*, not only the earlier Syriac and Latin versions, but also such other versions as the Sahidic and Bohairic, witness for inclusion.

more of empty space between Mark and Luke), in the scriptorium where this manuscript was copied it apparently was recognized that there was some question about how Mark should be ended.

From the fact that the scribe of B ends Mark at verse 8, followed by the ornament and the subscription κατὰ Μᾶρκον, but leaves the remainder of the column and the whole of the next column blank, Williams concludes: 'the scribe knew of the existence of a conclusion to the Gospel, which he did not feel authorized to copy... he considered the form of the Gospel which ended with v. 8 as the authentic one'. Included in Williams' argument is the fact that the space left blank is both more than required for the so-called 'shorter' ending for Mark, and less than required for the so-called 'longer' ending: namely Mk. 16: 9–20.[1]

A more correct inference would seem to be that the scribe knew that the Gospel did not end at 16: 8 in some manuscripts, but was not certain how it should end, or was producing a copy which could be ended according to the wishes of others. That the scribe considered the form of the Gospel which ended with 16: 8 as the authentic one, is by no means clear. He only knew that the text he was copying up to 16: 8 was largely undisputed, and that what if anything was to follow 16: 8 was a matter of dispute. By not copying anything beyond 16: 8 he met the essential requirement of those who felt the Gospel ended there; by leaving a blank space before copying the Gospel of Luke, he met the essential requirement of those who felt that the Gospel needed either an ending or some word of explanation following 16: 8. By including the ornament and subscription κατὰ Μᾶρκον after 16: 8, the scribe was 'finishing' his work. It could 'go out' of the scriptorium in this form. But any purchaser or user easily could have had the ornament and subscription erased and, in the space allowed, he could have ended the Gospel according to his own decision or he could have used it without alteration. The advantage of this form of the text is that it allows for some further treatment of a disputed matter. It is certainly copied in such a way that an ending may be added if desired. Why the space left blank is more than necessary for the shorter ending or less than needed for the longer ending is not entirely clear. It would seem to suggest, however, that those responsible

---

[1] Williams, 'The appendices', p. 358.

for the production of B did not envisage a use for it requiring the longer ending. All this is perfectly in keeping with a situation in which the longer ending is known, but disapproved, and where it is felt prudent to allow for something further to be written in the space left blank.

10. A PROPOSED CONJECTURAL SOLUTION

Were there conditions obtaining in Alexandria under which the last twelve verses could have been omitted from copies of Mark deliberately? In returning to Origen, as we seek to answer this question, we do not intend to suggest that he personally would have favoured omitting these verses. On the contrary. However, we return to him with real justification for the following reasons:

(1) A text type found in some of his New Testament citations is closely related to that common to B and ℵ, and, therefore, a text or texts at one time used by him may have omitted Mk. 16: 9–20.

(2) His admirer and biographer, Eusebius of Caesarea, may have preserved for us Origen's solutions to the questions posed by Marinus which we find in the text published by Mai.

(3) His position as head of the Catechetical School in Alexandria and his great interest in scriptural exegesis places him in a unique position to enable us through his writings to get our bearings with regard to the way a problem of this kind would have been faced in Alexandria after the fourfold Gospel canon had become fixed and after harmonies like that of Ammonius of Alexandria had been created.

Ammonius of Alexandria was a contemporary of Origen and his Harmony or Diatessaron Gospel belongs to the same world of imaginative and methodical scholarship as Origen's monumental Hexapla. Ammonius took the text of the Gospel of Matthew and then arranged on either side the parallel texts from Mark, Luke and John. This arrangement accords to Matthew a unique place among the four, not merely because the order of Matthew is thus made basic to the Harmony as a whole, but because such an arrangement made no provision for a comparison of passages parallel in the other Gospels but having no parallel in Matthew.

Origen approached the problem of reconciling discrepancies in parallel accounts between the Gospels according to a similar perspective. We have already seen this in the way he dealt with Celsus' derisive observation that the resurrected Lord showed himself but to a single woman, a point that is supported by both Mark and John. If one were to settle matters like this by counting witnesses, one would need to agree with Celsus, for according to Luke, Jesus showed himself to no women, according to Matthew he showed himself to two women, while according to Mark and John he showed himself to a single woman; indeed, she is identified in both as Mary Magdalene. But Origen did not approach the problem in this way. He simply says that Celsus is mistaken because, according to Matthew, Jesus showed himself to two women. This seems to suggest that in Alexandria there was a norm by which such discrepancies between Matthew and the other evangelists were settled; they were settled by adhering to the witness of Matthew even when Matthew was not supported by the other evangelists.

Ammonius' Diatessaron Gospel was the perfect tool for the task of harmonizing discrepancies between Matthew and the other three Gospels. In fact, that is the only practical purpose it could have served efficiently. It certainly could not have served as an adequate tool to facilitate harmonization of discrepancies between Mark and John or Mark and Luke, or Luke and John – except in those places where they had parallel passages which were also parallel to Matthew.

Such a handling of the source problem was peculiarly Alexandrian in spirit and method. Here a certain principle of economy was in operation where it was imagined that Matthew was the correct and adequate apostolic norm, and that the only decisive difficulties that could arise would be where the testimony of one or more of the other evangelists appeared to conflict with the witness of Matthew. Under such circumstances it would be highly desirable to have all the data conveniently arranged to facilitate the most careful examination of the exact wording of the parallel texts. This is precisely the need that Ammonius' Harmony met.

For purposes of contrast we may consider the corresponding

rationale for the quite different approach to the source problem in Tatian's Diatessaron and for the Eusebian system of Gospel cross-references. Both Tatian's Diatessaron and Eusebius' Sections–Canons system are based on an inclusive principle.[1]

Tatian's Diatessaron solves the source problem by creating a new Gospel on the inclusive principle. Almost everything that is in all four Gospels is included in Tatian's Diatessaron.[2] This solution was blocked eventually, however, and the Syrian church returned to the fourfold Gospel canon.

Eusebius solved the source problem by an ingenious method of dividing each Gospel into as many sections as were necessary for the purposes of comparison, numbering these sections consecutively from the beginning of each Gospel, and then classifying each section on the basis of whether the section concerned was unique to the Gospel concerned, or parallel to one or more of the other three. Thus if a section was represented in all four Gospels it had, in addition to its sequential number in the Gospel concerned, also the number I; if in Matthew, Mark, and Luke – II; Matthew, Luke, and John – III; Matthew, Mark, and John – IV; Matthew and Luke – V; Matthew and Mark – VI; Matthew and John – VII; Luke and Mark – VIII; Luke and John – IX; if unique to the Gospel concerned – X. Eusebius then constructed ten corresponding tables with the tenth having four separate divisions, one for each Gospel. By referring to the proper table it is possible to learn exactly where to go in any of the other Gospels to find the passage or passages parallel to any particular passage under consideration.

This system has the advantage of facilitating comparison of parallel passages without destroying the organic unity of any of the Gospels. Nonetheless Matthew is given a certain prominence in this system in that his order is invariably followed when any difference in sequential arrangement occurs. To this extent Eusebius' Canons show a kinship to Ammonius' Diatessaron Gospel, to which work in fact Eusebius gives credit for the idea of creating his own system.

Although Tatian's Diatessaron and Eusebius' Canons are both inclusive in nature, they give divergent testimony as to the

---

[1] Cf. Streeter, *Four Gospels*, pp. 122–3, who shows a consciousness of these two different principles at work.

[2] Tatian made some omissions, e.g. the genealogies.

last twelve verses of Mark. As we have noted, Tatian included these verses, whereas they have no place in Eusebius' Canons. In other words the last section in Mark to be included in the Canons of Eusebius is 233, which refers to Mk. 16: 8, which, having parallels in Matthew and Luke, is found in Canon II. Mk. 16: 9–20 includes sections parallel to Luke, John and Matthew, as well as sections unique to Mark. No provision, however, is made for any of these sections of Mark in Eusebius' Canons.

It has sometimes been assumed erroneously that the absence of Mk. 16: 9–20 from Eusebius' Canons means that they were omitted in Ammonius' Harmony. The relationship between these two works, however, does not warrant this assumption. Nonetheless, because Eusebius explicitly says that it was Ammonius' Diatessaron Gospel which afforded him the idea for his system of cross-references, we are justified in considering the possibility that these verses were absent from that work.

Only the entire text of one Gospel was included in Ammonius' Harmony – and that was the text of Matthew. Thus by far the greater part of John, a large part of Luke, and a considerable portion of Mark would not have been included. The principle to be followed was clear: if the section in question in Mark, Luke, or John had a parallel to a section in Matthew, then that section was copied in one of the margins alongside its parallel section in Matthew. According to this principle Mk. 16: 1 would not have been included, but Mk. 16: 2–8 would. What followed verse 8 in the text of Mark would have had a very questionable status in Ammonius' Diatessaron Gospel. It could have been omitted on the principle of economy on the grounds that aside from the possible exception of verse 15 no part of Mk. 16: 9–20 has a clear parallel in Matthew. Mk. 16: 9–20 has clear parallels to the post-resurrection stories in the other Gospels and Acts, and it is generally held that these verses were conflated out of these earlier accounts; but the fact that these parallels are largely confined to Luke–Acts and John is generally overlooked. By indirection Mk. 16: 9–20 witnesses with Luke and John against Matthew in their resurrection narratives. The significance of this for the present discussion is that the only part of Mk. 16: 9–20 which in any case could have been included in

Ammonius' Diatessaron Gospel would have been less than a dozen words in Mk. 16: 15.

It is quite possible, therefore, that the last section of Mark to be included in Ammonius' Diatessaron Gospel would have been Mk. 16: 2–8.

Even so, the omission of the last twelve verses of Mark from Ammonius' Diatessaron Gospel would not explain their omission from Eusebius' Canons, since everything in Luke's Gospel after 24: 9 (forty-four verses), and everything in John after 20: 23 (the whole of chapter 21 and the last seven verses of chapter 20), have no parallel in Matthew and would have been omitted from Ammonius' Diatessaron Gospel, and yet these portions of Luke and John are accounted for in the Canons of Eusebius. It follows that the presence or absence of Mk. 16: 9–20 from Ammonius' Diatessaron Gospel would not explain the fact that there is no provision for it in the Canons of Eusebius.[1]

And yet if we retrace the thought processes that would have governed the decision whether to include or exclude Mk. 16: 9–20 in a harmony like that of Ammonius, we will see how a question concerning the authenticity of these verses could have arisen. This does not mean that we are reduced to suggesting that it was Ammonius who first raised a question about the authenticity of these verses. It is only that in rethinking the

---

[1] The Eusebian Canons make no provision for passages found only in Mark and John but not in Matthew and Luke, and no provision for passages found in Mark, Luke and John, but not in Matthew, presumably because they were not felt to be needed. An agreement between Mark and Luke like Jesus appearing to two men as they were walking in the country could have been included in the Canons of Eusebius. But an agreement between Mark and John, like Jesus appearing to Mary Magdalene, would have necessitated the creation of a new Canon with perhaps only a single entry. Such considerations as this and the fact that Mk. 16: 9–20 as a whole would have been very difficult to apportion among the Canons of Eusebius must be kept in mind as one ponders the significance of all this for the problem of the authenticity of these verses. Bellinzoni's discoveries (*Sayings of Jesus*, pp. 140–2) regarding the existence in the second century of catechetical materials harmonized out of the Gospels (materials which were known to Justin, Clement of Alexandria, the author of the Pseudo-Clementine Homilies, and Origen), deserves careful attention. He notes that these sources never derive material from Mark or John, and that the main difference between these harmonized materials and Tatian's Diatessaron is Tatian's use of John. The Eusebian Canons and Ammonius' Harmony need restudy in the light of these discoveries.

problem he faced at this particular point in the production of his Diatessaron Gospel, we are confronted in principle by the problem that Origen would have faced in considering the relation of Mk. 16: 9–20 – not in the first place to the rest of Mark, but rather to the witness of the Gospels as a whole with *Matthew regarded as the apostolic norm.*

Mk. 16: 9–20 constituted one integral lectionary reading. It is important that this lectionary reading began with verse 9 and that another lection (that for the second Sunday after Easter) ended with verse 8. It is conceivable, therefore, that in the early church there were manuscripts which were marked so that a reader could know where to end and where to begin these lectionary readings.[1] With or without a scribal mark for this purpose, providing there were other compelling reasons to omit this ending to Mark, it would have been natural to choose to make the break after ἐφοβοῦντο γάρ and before ἀναστάς. For it is here that more than one of the classical discrepancies between the evangelists begins. There were other discrepancies. For example, in Matt. 28: 8 we read: 'And they departed quickly from the sepulchre with fear and great joy; *and did run to bring His disciples word*', while in Mk. 16: 8 we read: 'And they went out quickly, and fled from the sepulchre; for they trembled and were amazed: *neither said they anything to any man*; for they were afraid.' Thus if an omission was to be made, why might it not just as well have included verse 8? This is a valid question and stands in the way of a convincing case for any view that narrowly conceives this as a problem of omission caused by discrepancies. But if there are *other* considerations arguing for omission of certain verses coming later, it would be difficult to argue that there was a *better* point at which to start the omission than with ἀναστάς. For with 16: 9 a complex of difficulties confronts the exegete. Here, for example, the testimony of Paul in 1 Cor. 15: 5, where the appearance of Jesus to Peter is mentioned first in what appears to be a sequential series of appearances, seems to be in conflict with Mark's statements that Jesus first appeared to Mary Magdalene. And as has been shown, it is precisely with ἀναστάς that a particularly troublesome dis-

[1] Burgon, *Last Twelve Verses*, pp. 212ff., seeks to account for the original omission of these verses as due to a scribal misunderstanding of such a lectionary rubric.

crepancy between Matthew and Mark occurs. And the reader does not proceed another step forward in the text of Mark before he encounters a third difficulty. For after the reference to Mary Magdalene there is no reference to another woman and certainly no reference to Jesus appearing to another woman. Yet Origen was prepared to appeal to the account of Matthew where Jesus showed himself to *two* women – as if what stood in Mark was not even to be considered. That in this difference between Matthew and Mark, John agreed with Mark, and that Origen deigned not even to acknowledge this fact but peremptorily contradicted Celsus on the authority of Matthew alone; all this suggests something of the difficulties concentrated in Mk. 16: 9. Perhaps we should also add as a further difficulty in verse 9 the reference to Mary Magdalene as a woman who had once been possessed with demons.[1]

But because such discrepancies and difficulties are not peculiar to verse 9, though they seem unusually concentrated there, they could never by themselves account for the omission of the *whole* of Mk. 16: 9–20. Such a radical action, so uncongenial to the 'faithful' and 'circumspect' as the text published by Mai indicates, requires an objectionable exegetical surd that reaches beneath the level of questions like 'what happened?' or 'when did it happen?', and, striking at the vital centre of the church's life,[2] threatens its very existence. The kind of threat, for example, that was represented in such second-century sectarian phenomena as the Montanist Movement.

Mk. 16: 9–20 contains promises of Jesus to which the church has never succeeded in accommodating itself, except by unconscious repression. Most Christians do not know what these verses teach. They are seldom if ever expounded from the pulpit and almost never appealed to in didactic circumstances. Christians have long since learned to live with these promises by paying them no attention and to regard all efforts to take them seriously as bizarre acts of unfaith on the part of ignorant or misguided sectarians. But at what period and under what

[1] Cf. above, p. 31, n. 2
[2] Striking at the confidence and trust the church has in the promises of her Lord, striking at the closely related confidence in her clergy and bishops, and also striking at the pulsating level of concern for what is edifying for the children of God.

THE LAST TWELVE VERSES OF MARK

circumstances was the church successful in repressing the troublesome teaching contained in these verses? And how were the problems created for the church by these verses dealt with in the early church?

In the eighth book of the *Apostolic Constitutions*, in the opening section, Mk. 16: 17–18 is cited and discussed. This discussion reads as follows:

These gifts were first bestowed on us the apostles when we were about to preach the gospel to every creature, and afterwards were of necessity afforded to those who had by our means believed; not for the advantage of those who performed them, but for the conviction of the unbelievers...It is not therefore necessary that every one of the faithful should cast out demons, or raise the dead, or speak with tongues; but such an one only who is vouchsafed this gift...Now we say these things, that those who have received such gifts may not exalt themselves against those who have not received them... Let not, therefore, anyone who works signs and wonders judge any one of the faithful who is not vouchsafed the same: for the gifts of God which are bestowed by Him through Christ are various; and one man receives one gift, and another another. For perhaps one has the word of wisdom, and another the word of knowledge; another discerning of spirits; another, foreknowledge of things to come; another, the word of teaching; another long suffering; another, continence according to the law: for even Moses, the man of God, when he wrought signs in Egypt, did not exalt himself against his equals...Nor did Joshua...though he had made the sun stand still...exult insolently over Phineas or Caleb...Neither did the wise Daniel who was twice delivered from the mouths of the lions, nor the three children who were delivered from the furnace of fire, despise the rest of their fellow Israelites: for they knew that they had not escaped these terrible miseries by their own might; but by the power of God did they both work miracles, and were delivered from miseries...Neither is everyone that prophesies holy, nor every one that casts out devils religious...Wherefore if among you also there be a man or a woman, and such an one obtains any gift, let him be humble, that God may be pleased with him. For the Lord says: 'Upon whom will I look, but upon him that is humble and quiet, and trembles at my word?'[1]

After concluding the discussion in this way, the following section is introduced as follows:

We have now finished the first part of this discourse concerning gifts, whatever they be, which God has bestowed upon men according to his own will...But now our discourse hastens on to the principal part, that is, the constitution of ecclesiastical affairs.[2]

Then follows a prescription of how bishops are to be selected and ordained. This ordination ceremony is ended with an ex-

---

[1] *ANF*, VII, 479–81.   [2] *ANF*, VII, 481.

hortation to the people from the new bishop. Whereupon the deacon announces that all the unbelievers present are to leave, and once silence reigns he petitions the faithful to pray in turn for the following groups: the catechumens, the demon-possessed, the initiates, and the penitents. The newly ordained bishop offers a special blessing for each group, and the deacon dismisses each group before calling the next forward. In the case of the demon-possessed, the bishop (the afflicted with bowed heads before him) exorcizes with this prayer: 'Thou only begotten God, the son of the great Father, rebuke these wicked spirits, and deliver the works of thy hands from the power of the adverse spirit. For to Thee is due glory, honour, and worship, and by Thee to thy Father, in the Holy Spirit, for ever. Amen.'[1]

After the services for the special groups the deacon leads the whole congregation in a general prayer which begins as follows:

Let us pray for the peace and happy settlement of the world, and of the holy churches; that the God of the whole world may afford us his everlasting peace, and such as may not be taken away from us; that He may preserve us in a full prosecution of such virtue as is according to godliness. Let us pray for the holy catholic and apostolic church which is spread from one end of the earth to the other; that God would preserve and keep it unshaken, and free from the waves of this life, until the end of the world, as founded upon a rock; for the holy parish in this place, that the lord of the whole world may vouchsafe us without failure to follow after his heavenly hope, and without ceasing to pay Him the debt of our prayer. Let us pray for every episcopacy which is under the whole heaven, of those that rightly divide the word of Thy truth.[2]

Through this document we are enabled to see one way in which the church was able to deal with the troublesome influence of the teaching contained in Mk. 16: 17–18. This was the way of containment. The authenticity of the promises is accepted. However, by citing precedents from the Old Testament scriptures, and by introducing the teaching of the apostle Paul on spiritual gifts, the normative character of the teaching of these verses is nullified, and the peace and order of the church is maintained under the authority of properly ordained bishops who are formal custodians of the apostolic gifts of casting out demons and laying on of hands, with no provision being made for speaking in tongues and picking up serpents – these gifts by

[1] *ANF*, vii, 484. [2] *ANF*, vii, 485.

default being left to those who have them, with the admonition that they do not elevate the possessor above the rest of the faithful.

Still another way to nullify the disruptive character of the literal teaching of these verses was by allegorizing and spiritualizing their meaning.

In his attack on Christianity Porphyry (or the pagan philosopher who popularized Porphyry's work) based one of his objections on the saying: 'If they shall drink any deadly thing, it shall not hurt them.'

He wrote as follows:

Again, consider in detail that other passage, where He says, 'Such signs shall follow them that believe; they shall lay hands upon sick folk, and they shall recover, and if they drink any deadly drug, it shall in no wise hurt them.' So the right thing would be for those selected for the priesthood, and particularly those who claim to the episcopate or presidency, to make use of this form of test. The deadly drug should be set before them in order that the man who received no harm from the drinking of it might be given precedence of the rest. And if they are not bold enough to accept this sort of test, they ought to confess that they do not believe in the things Jesus said. For if it is a peculiarity of the faith to overcome the evil of a poison and to remove the pain of a sick man, the believer who does not do these things either has not become a genuine believer, or else, though his belief is genuine, the thing that he believes in is not potent but feeble.

To this the apologist represented in *The Apocriticus of Macarius Magnes* responds:

We must not take the words about the sickness and the 'deadly drug' in too literal a sense. Otherwise we shall find them contradicted by two facts. First, those who are unbelievers may likewise recover from deadly drugs, so that the recovery need not consist in whether men are believers or not, but in the power of the drug. Secondly, many unbelievers run away at the first sign of sickness, but we must not therefore argue that those who stay to tend the sick are believers in consequence. Such literal and manward tests will not do, or we shall have people boasting of their faith simply because they have some skill in nursing.

So the 'deadly drug' must be taken in a less literal sense. Then follows an allegorical interpretation based on something said by Paul. At this point the apologist turns to the matter of laying hands on the sick:

'Laying hands on the sick' must have a similar spiritual explanation. Their 'hands' are their practical energies, and the 'sick' are changes in the seasons, which are often sick through such things as storms, or want of rain.

68

Certainly Polycarp is an example of this, for while he exercised the office of bishop at Smyrna, the season of standing crops was greatly sick, when the heaven was not concealed by the smallest cloud, and poured down from the sky a burning heat, scorching to a great degree the vast tracts of land that lay beneath it; and it dried up the moisture of the foliage, and the trouble caused no little difficulty to men. Then that great man of God came, and when he saw the inhabitants thus afflicted, he in a sense laid his hands by means of prayer upon the burnt-up season, and suddenly made all things well. And later, when the land was drowned with unlimited rain, and the dwellers in it were in a pitiable state of distress, this same Polycarp stretched his hands into the air and dispelled the calamity, by healing that which was hateful to them. And indeed, before he became bishop, when he was managing a widow's house, wheresoever he laid on his hands in faith, all things were well. And why should I stay to speak of the blessings conferred on men by Irenaeus of Lugdunum, or Fabian of Rome, or Cyprian of Carthage? Passing them by, I will say something about men of today. How many, by stretching forth their hands in prayer to the heavenly Ruler, for the invisible diseases of suffering which press grievously upon the souls of men, have healed the afflicted invisibly in ways we know not? How many by the laying on of their hands have caused to be well those catechumens who were in their former fever of transgression or disease, raising them to the new blessing of health through the divine and mystical leaven [i.e. baptism]? For the responsibility that is laid upon the faithful is not so much zeal in driving away the sufferings of the body (for God knows that these things discipline in man, rather than overthrow, the government of his soul), as those things which are wont to harm the understanding by enslaving the judgment of the reason.[1]

Here again the authenticity of Mk. 16: 9–20 is not in question. But the literal meaning of the text presents obvious difficulties. And rather than meet the telling arguments of his opponent, the apologist detours around the problem by appeal to allegory, and spiritual interpretation, and gives an explanation of the promises of Jesus which is more in accord with the experience of the church. Allegory was particularly utilized by Origen in cases where otherwise discrepancies or dogmatic difficulties would have confronted the exegete.[2]

Origen used allegory, for example, in meeting the dogmatic arguments put forward by some for omitting the parable of the Rich Man and Lazarus.[3] Again in reference to the difficulty of reconciling Matt. 12: 40 with Lk. 23: 43, Origen notes that this discrepancy so distresses some people 'that they make bold to

---

[1] T. W. Crafer (trans.), *The Apocriticus of Macarius Magnes*, Translations of Christian Literature, Ser. I, Greek Texts (London, 1919), pp. 85–8.
[2] Pack, 'Methodology', p. 143.   [3] Commentary on John 32. 13.

suppose that the words, "Today shalt thou be with me in the Paradise of God", were an addition to the Gospel made by some unscrupulous hand'. By appeal first to a 'simpler' sense and then a 'deeper' sense of the text, Origen is enabled to circumvent the difficulty. Here we see Origen meeting difficulties that others met in a different way to him, in these cases at least, an unnecessarily radical way, i.e. by omission. But in the second century omission would not have appeared so radical as it did in the third, and in Alexandria it would have been regarded as a progressive measure if it removed the basis for ridicule of the gods and served an edifying purpose for the community. An example has just been given of the way in which the Christian's faith or lack of faith in the power of their Lord could be ridiculed by appeal to Mk. 16: 18. By the use of allegory such ridicule could be met by finding hidden and edifying meanings in the text. But it is unlikely that the Porphyrys would be silenced by such explanations. And in any case, as the passage in Book VIII of the *Apostolic Constitutions* makes clear, there were some Christians who believed literally in these promises, and would not have been interested in having them allegorized. They so prized the possession of these gifts as signs that the Lord was working with *them* that they disturbed the order and peace of the church.

A third way of dealing with these problems, therefore, would have been to suppress the verses by omitting them from some copies. Even the most faithful of Christians are not immune from the ill effects of drinking deadly poisons. This is so patently true that many if not all reasonable men must have had serious doubts about these promises. But to doubt these promises in the early church was not to doubt the trustworthy character of Jesus Christ or to doubt the power of God, but to question the apostolic origin of the text in which these promises were found: they were found at the end of Mark, in a section which, not discounting other possible difficulties, began with a verse in conflict with the apostolic norm (i.e. Matthew) at two points. If to this are added the kind of difficulties reflected in Book VIII of the *Apostolic Constitutions*, it is possible to see how the practice of ending Mark with ἐφοβοῦντο γάρ could have arisen, and once in being, how manuscripts with this reading could have become current in some locales and remained in circulation until difficulties fed by those verses no longer posed a threat to the order, peace and well being of the church.

'Faithful' and 'circumspect' teachers like Origen generally speaking would not have argued for the omission of a textual reading that had been received in the church. But insofar as they were trained in the ways of Alexandrian text criticism *and had a concern for what was edifying for the church* they would have tended to respect received exemplars which omitted this kind of doubtful reading, and in some situations could have tolerated and perhaps even approved the production and use of copies of Mark ending with ἐφοβοῦντο γάρ. This would help explain the fact that the Cappadocian Fathers, all of whom were of the Alexandrian school, make no reference to Mk. 16: 9–20. And further, because of the influence of the Cappadocians on the Armenian church, it would help explain why the Armenian version omitted these verses. In this way a theory of textual development can be posited which accounts for most of the evidence bearing on the question of the external witnesses for and against the authenticity of the last twelve verses of Mark.

This text tradition may have originated in the time of Origen, though this seems less likely than that its beginnings are pre-Origenian. Zuntz's conclusion bears repeating at this point: 'In the latter half of the second century the Alexandrian bishopric possessed a scriptorium, which by its output set the standard for the Alexandrian type of Biblical manuscript.' The close similarity between the texts of P75 and B in balance weighs heavily for the earlier origin of the B ℵ text. Since Origen, for a time at least, used this text, it is probable that this use increased its prestige in circles influenced by him.

Origen is important for an understanding of this whole development: (1) not because he would have favoured omission, but because he probably would have advocated remaining open to this omission as a hypothetical possibility (as per Mai's text?); (2) because his writings as a whole illuminate the situation in Alexandria in the archaic period (late phase perhaps) of this conjectured development; and (3) also because his own travel and influence throughout the church help us to see something of the attraction and spread of the methods of Alexandrian scholarship.

If in fact the text tradition witnessing for omission owes its origin in part to the influence of Alexandrian scholarship, then the eventual triumph of the text tradition for inclusion would have a significant parallel in the development of the Homeric manuscript tradition. 'The influence of the great Alexandrian critics – Zenodotus, Aristophanes of Byzantium and Aristarchus – on culture generally, and especially on schools, must not be exaggerated. All the manuscripts of the *Iliad* and the *Odyssey* show that their advice went unheeded, except for a slight effect upon our Vulgate and the papyri. The Greek literary tradition was particularly conservative and hidebound, and it resisted all the efforts of the learned men at the museum to introduce "cuts" – "atheteses" of the lines which they considered should be expurgated.'[1]

This is not an argument for the authenticity of Mk. 16: 9–20. Rather it points out that if these verses were known as a part of the received textual tradition in Alexandria at some time in the second century, and if some time later, but still before the end of the second century, under the influence of Alexandrian textual criticism (along with whatever other factors pressing for omission may have been at work), they were 'expurgated' from some or all copies of Mark made at some important Alexandrian scriptorium, then the fate of this Alexandrian effort to introduce a 'cut' is similar to the fate of the Alexandrian efforts in Homeric criticism. Needless to say, the question of the validity of the Alexandrian efforts to 'expurgate' texts is not settled by the fact that their advice went largely unheeded. This means that even if Mk. 16: 9–20 were expurgated in some Alexandrian copies of Mark it is an open question whether there might not have been valid literary grounds recognized at that time which argued against the authenticity of these verses, and which led to a critical judgment that they should not be copied. This question can only be settled by a study of the internal evidence, beginning with an analysis of the linguistic, stylistic, and conceptional character of these verses in comparison with the rest of Mark. Meanwhile, it must be held as a possibility that the verses (*a*) are *not* original but (*b*) were added after the composition of other Gospels (in part drawing on them) and (*c*) that an attempt was made (unsuccessfully) in the Alexandrian tradition to restore the original state of affairs.

[1] Marrou, *History of Education*, p. 164.

Weighing against this possibility, however, and weighing in favour of the verses being original to Mark, is the fact that while a fairly credible account can be given for the origin of the textual tradition for omission, no very satisfactory explanation has ever been given for the undeniably early and widespread witness for inclusion of these verses on the assumption that they are not original but a later addition to the text of Mark.

B. H. Streeter in *The Four Gospels* asserts that the distribution of the manuscripts and versions, taken in connection with the witness of Eusebius, 'compels' [*sic*] one to assume that the last twelve verses of Mark were missing from the first copies that reached Africa, Alexandria, Caesarea, and Antioch (p. 336).

Streeter did not specify what he meant in referring to the 'distribution' of manuscripts and versions. But if his own classification of primary, secondary and tertiary authorities for local texts be made a testing ground for verification, it would be necessary at best to read the evidence selectively in order to agree with this conclusion (cf. p. 52). As Kenneth Clark has noted, the earliest versions – Latin, Syriac and Coptic – all witness for inclusion. And on the basis of the current discussion of text types, except for the Alexandrian or Beta text type, all other textual groups on balance seem to witness for inclusion (p. 58).

Moreover, Streeter's theory that the last twelve verses of Mark are the result of an attempt to harmonize conflicting resurrection traditions (p. 359) and his suggestion that the text tradition for including these verses originated in Rome in the first half of the second century (p. 353), while plausible enough in their own right, take no account of the practical difficulties inherent in the teaching contained in these verses, and afford no explanation for how these verses (be they not original) could have become so widely and *uniformly* accepted in the early church.

As Streeter himself writes in another connection: 'All our evidence as to the history of the Church during the first two centuries' points to the lack of 'a highly centralized organization' able to enforce or secure uniformity in the text of the Gospels (p. 342). There is no evidence that the church in Rome had either the power or the inclination to promote widespread adoption of these verses. The church in Rome may have found useful scriptures in which an effort was made to harmonize conflicting traditions. But there is nothing in the history of the church at Rome that would give reason to think that that church would have favoured or promoted the addition of an ending to Mark which represents the risen Lord as explicitly instructing the apostles that if they have faith they will be able to pick up serpents and drink poison without harmful effects.

Our study leads us to conclude that the text tradition for inclusion, unlike that for omission, cannot be traced to any particular ecclesiastical centre or geographical locale, nor to any singular text type or textual group.

When the critic ponders the practical difficulties inherent in the teaching of these verses, it only serves to magnify the problem of comprehending in a convincing way how, i.e. under what circumstances, this ending could ever have been added to copies of Mark and thereafter achieve the widespread acceptance attested by early patristic and versional witnesses. This problem, often overlooked, or passed over lightly by those who favour omission, actually poses an historical difficulty of considerable magnitude for any theory which presupposes that these verses were not original but added after the composition of other Gospels.

II. A TENTATIVE CONCLUSION

Our tentative conclusion in the light of all these findings is as follows: while a study of the external evidence is rewarding in itself and can be very illuminating in many ways, and while it enables us to understand how the practice of omission might have arisen, it does not produce the evidential grounds for a definitive solution to the problem. A study of the history of the text, *by itself*, has not proven sufficient, since the evidence is divided and the decisive period, namely the second century, remains at present largely shrouded in obscurity. We can only say with certainty (concerning Mk. 16: 9–20 in this period) that manuscripts including these verses were circulating in the second century. Whether there were also manuscripts ending with ἐφοβοῦντο γάρ circulating in this archaic period, we do not know. It may be conjectured with some reason that such manuscripts were circulating *in Egypt* by the end of the second century. There is nothing to support a conjecture that such manuscripts were circulating outside Egypt this early. The presumption that the autograph of Mark ended at ἐφοβοῦντο γάρ is dependent, at least in part, on a widespread belief that a careful study of the linguistic, stylistic and conceptional character of Mk. 16: 9–20 indicates that these verses do not belong with the rest of the Gospel. To what extent this is due to a circular argument which falsely presupposes that the manuscript evidence is decisively against the authenticity of these verses is difficult to say. In any case it will be necessary to consider the internal evidence bearing on this question before further conclusions can be drawn.

PART TWO
THE INTERNAL EVIDENCE

Part One of this study of the traditional ending of Mark indicates that the external evidence, in the last analysis, is inconclusive. How does the internal evidence weigh? Does it clearly indicate that the last twelve verses of Mark were not written by the author of the rest of that Gospel? Or is there clear evidence that the same hand was at work in the composition and/or editing of both parts? Or as with the external evidence does the internal evidence leave the student without sufficient grounds for taking a strong position one way or the other on this question?

Most exhaustive studies of the vocabulary, style, and grammar of Mk. 16: 9–20 have been made by scholars who have wished to disprove the assertions of their opponents that the diction of these verses proves their unauthenticity. In general these efforts have succeeded in blunting if not refuting the specific linguistic arguments put forth by those arguing for the omission of these verses. However, in no case have either the advocates of omission or the advocates of inclusion presented the evidence as a whole. Each has selected his evidence in accordance with a view he was defending. This is no less true of a recent treatment of this question made by Robert Morgenthaler.[1]

Morgenthaler wishes to demonstrate that 'word-statistical research leads to clear results'. He assumes that his readers are convinced on textual grounds that these verses do not belong to Mark, and he believes that these readers will be impressed with the way in which his 'word-statistical research' supports this view, and will accordingly take 'word-statistical research' more seriously. Actually, Morgenthaler only succeeds in demonstrating how misleading such statistical research can be. For example he considers πορεύεσθαι and concludes that it would be 'really amazing' for Mark to use this word three times in this ending in an uncompounded form since he elsewhere uses

[1] *Statistik des neutestamentlichen Wortschatzes* (Zürich, 1958), pp. 58–60.

compounds so readily. But as is shown in the following study, once one considers the matter contextually it is not at all 'amazing' that the uncompounded forms would be used in these three instances.

Again when Morgenthaler utilizes his 'tables of words pre-ferred by Mark' to test this question he finds that the un-authenticity of these verses is 'emphatically confirmed'. But this only points up the inadequacy of such tables. For example, it is characteristic of Mark to use λόγος and εὐαγγέλιον abso-lutely. Both these words are found in Mk. 16: 9–20. Yet Mor-genthaler's tables make no reference to these very important words which, as used by Mark, entail distinctive theological concepts.

When Morgenthaler considers his grammatical statistics he notes that Mark uses the dative plural αὐτοῖς and εἰ μή and ἵνα especially often. He finds that αὐτοῖς appears three times in Mk. 16: 9–20; while εἰ μή and ἵνα are 'totally lacking'. Such facts by themselves mean very little. What would be important would be to show that εἰ μή and ἵνα are not used in these verses where they appropriately could have been used. Then the sig-nificance of such phenomena would be greatly increased if it could be shown that what is used in place of these grammatical phenomena in Mk. 16: 9–20 is elsewhere avoided in Mark. And the value of this kind of evidence is further enhanced if it can be shown that in the synoptic parallels where Mark prefers these other words, Matthew and Luke sometimes use εἰ μή and ἵνα.

Morgenthaler notes that as far as compound words are con-cerned the frequency with which they occur indicates that Mk. 16: 9–20 belongs with Mark, Luke and Paul as over against the rest of the New Testament. But instead of acknowledging that this weighs in favour of 16: 9–20 belonging with the rest of Mark, he blunts the force of what is for his case an anomaly by ob-serving: 'With the many compounds in the concluding section – it is most astonishing to find the simple πορεύεσθαι.'

Morgenthaler observes that Mark likes foreign words, and then notes: 'In this section, however, no foreign word emerges. That can be an accident, but it certainly does not speak for authenticity of this section.' The implication of this way of stating the matter is that the absence of foreign words in Mk. 16: 9–20, however slightly, does weigh against the authenticity

of these verses. But for such a consideration to have any probative value it would be necessary to know whether Mark's liking
for foreign words is such as to lead to the expectation that in any
twelve verses of Mark one would likely find one or more foreign
words. A further refinement of this kind of test would require
the determination whether Mark's liking of foreign words is
such as to lead one to expect their being found in a section like
Mk. 16: 9–20. Morgenthaler acknowledges that nothing can be
maintained with certainty regarding the authenticity of 16:
9–20 on the basis of the frequency and distribution of foreign
words in Mark, 'because the section in question is too short'.
The question is whether, and if so, under what circumstances, it
would be possible to maintain *anything* with *any meaningful degree*
of probability about the authenticity of these verses because of
the relative shortness of this section.

Morgenthaler notes that the use of the article could speak for
the authenticity of these verses. But he immediately contrasts
the case with the use of καί. The frequency with which καί is
used in Mk. 16: 9–20 is 'on the average' half what it is elsewhere
in Mark.

On the other hand, δέ is used over twice as often in 16: 9–20
as in the rest of Mark. Morgenthaler concludes that this 'certainly speaks for the unauthenticity' of Mk. 16: 9–20. He notes
that these frequencies vary in different parts of Mark and
recommends consulting the curves at the back of his book where
he has charted these frequencies. These curves indicate the
frequency with which four phenomena (the article, καί, αὐτός
and δέ) occur throughout the New Testament writings. In the
case of Mark it is shown that the article and αὐτός are used in
16: 9–20 with a frequency reasonably compatible with the rest
of that Gospel. They, therefore, call for no special comment.
The curves for καί and δέ, however, indicate something very
interesting. The use of καί is greater in the first half of Mark than
in the second, while the use of δέ is greater in the second half of
Mark than in the first. This means that the lower frequency of
καί in 16: 9–20 is in keeping with a tendency in the second half
of Mark. And the higher frequency of δέ in these verses is also
in keeping with a tendency in the second half of Mark.

One can even find sections in the second half of Mark where
the distribution of καί and δέ closely approximates the distribu-

tion in 16: 9–20 (where καί occurs nine times and δέ six). In 10: 13–24 καί occurs ten times and δέ eight. Similarly in 10: 32–40 καί occurs ten times and δέ eight. In Mk. 15: 1–15 καί occurs eight times and δέ twelve times, while immediately following in 15: 16–30 καί occurs sixteen times and δέ twice.

Obviously Mark can use καί and δέ with the same frequency and in the same proportions as obtains in 16: 9–20. And he is even capable of making sudden and radical shifts from one pattern of distribution to that of another. Morgenthaler attempts to refine his data by making a distinction between καί used at the beginning of a sentence and καί used elsewhere in a sentence. He notes that in the twelve verses preceding 16: 9 and in 1: 4–13 the use of καί to begin a sentence is significantly higher (in comparison to the total number of times καί is used in those sections) than is the case in 16: 9–20. Only once out of the nine times καί is used in 16: 9–20 does it begin a sentence.

Morgenthaler is mistaken, however, when he writes in this connection: 'A style is written here completely different than appears anywhere else in Mark's Gospel.' In Mk. 10: 32–40, for example, the ten occurrences of καί include only two which begin sentences. In 10: 23–31 καί occurs eleven times. Only once is it used to begin a sentence.

Yet Morgenthaler argues that since only once is καί used to begin a sentence out of the nine times it occurs in 16: 9–20, 'That alone is a circumstance which places in question the entire authenticity (*ganze Echtheit*) of Mk. 16: 9–20.' The fact is, it is not uncommon for Mark to use καί frequently in a section of his Gospel where most of the sentences are begun with a postpositive δέ as in 16: 9–20. For example, Morgenthaler took a section of Mark preceding 16: 9, i.e. 15: 46 – 16: 8, and noted that eight out of the sixteen times καί is used in those verses it is used to begin a sentence. But in a corresponding section immediately preceding 15: 46 (i.e. 15: 35–45) καί occurs fourteen times and is used only twice to begin a sentence. If one begins with δέ in verse 39, which corresponds grammatically with the way in which 16: 9 begins, the next nine uses of καί include only one instance where καί is used to begin a sentence. In fact καί is used twelve times after 15: 39 before it is used a second time to begin a sentence. At 15: 4 Mark reads for three verses before a sentence begins with καί, and then there are eight more verses where post-positive δέ is used to begin as many sentences before καί is used again to begin a sentence.

It is indeed the case that καί is used with great frequency to begin sentences in Mark, especially in the early chapters. But it is not true that the use of καί and δέ in 16: 9–20 is 'completely different than appears anywhere else in Mark's Gospel'. In fact the use of καί and δέ in 16: 9–20 is quite in keeping with usage in certain other parts of Mark, especially in the later chapters.

This concludes the evidence treated by Morgenthaler. His own conclusion deserves quoting: 'Now we have tested the whole section of Mk. 16: 9–20 word-statistically on all sides regarding its authenticity. Indications for authenticity are practically nonexistent. On the other hand the indications of unauthenticity are so numerous and so weighty, that one ought to draw the conclusion that Mk. 16: 9–20, judged on word-statistical evidence, could never have been written by the same hand as the rest of the Gospel of Mark.'

The need for a more complete study of the data is clear. The notes contained in the examination of the data which follows are often quite detailed and sometimes uneven in interest and importance. Some readers may feel that these notes should have been relegated to an appendix. The decision to include them in the text is based on the fact that they are integral to the investigation and essential to the overall argument of this book. However, if the reader chooses to proceed directly to the concluding paragraphs of this examination (p. 103), and then to the conclusions in Part Three, he may return to these notes with perhaps greater interest and appreciation.

2. AN EXAMINATION OF THE DICTION OF MK. 16: 9–20 WITH SPECIAL REFERENCE TO THE QUESTION OF THE RELATIONSHIP OF THESE VERSES TO THE REST OF MARK

Verse 9

The unexpressed subject of this sentence is Jesus, who is not mentioned by name until verse 19, though he is referred to constantly in verses 9–14. It is not unusual for Mark on occasion to use sparingly the name Jesus and its equivalents. It is missing in

1: 21 *b* after 1: 21 *a*, and in 1: 30 – 2: 4 after 1: 29, and in the whole of 3: 8 – 5: 20, where the actors and speakers change several times.

ʼΑναστάς   Mark uses this word fairly often, and several times to refer to resurrection (1: 35; 2: 14; 3: 26; 5: 42; 7: 24; 8: 31*; 9: 9*, 10*, 27, 31*; 10: 1, 34*; 12: 23*, 25*; 14: 57, 60. Passages marked with asterisk use word to refer to resurrection).

A participle followed by δέ is found in 2: 20; 6: 16; 9: 25; 10: 14; 15: 36, 39.

πρωΐ   In comparison to other N.T. writers, Mark seems to have a liking for this word. Cf. Mk. 1: 35; 11: 20; 13: 35; 15: 1; 16: 2.

πρώτῃ σαββάτου   The more usual way to refer to the first day of the week was to use μία σαββάτου (cf. 1 Cor. 16: 2), or μία σαββάτων (cf. Acts 20: 7; Lk. 24: 1; Matt. 28: 1). Mark follows this more usual usage in 16: 2 where his text is parallel to Matt. 28: 1 and Lk. 24: 1. But the use of πρώτη instead of μιᾷ is quite in keeping with τῇ πρώτῃ ἡμέρᾳ τῶν ἀζύμων in 14: 12. His use of the plural of σαββάτου in 16: 2, while the singular is used here, remains unexplained. With this one exception there does not seem to be any reason to question the Marcan character of the opening phrase: ʼΑναστὰς δὲ πρωΐ πρώτῃ σαββάτου. If Mark did compose the whole of 1: 1 – 16: 20, a simple explanation for the use of the plural of σαββάτου in one verse and the singular a few verses later would be to assume that he was following different sources, or that at one place he was closely following a source, while at the other he was using a form of the expression that was more natural to him.

ἐφάνη   This word used with reference to a person 'appearing' after death is not found frequently in the N.T. It occurs in this sense in Lk. 9: 8 with reference to Elijah and is not found in the Marcan parallel (Mk. 6: 15). There would be nothing unusual about Mark using it in 16: 9 and not in 6: 15. Note that though Luke uses it in 9: 8 he does not use it in chapter 24 with reference to an appearance of Jesus, but chooses rather the passive of ὁράω (24: 34). Interestingly enough, Luke does use φαίνω once more in his Gospel, i.e. in 24: 11; this time in a quite different sense, as a synonym of δοκέω, as also does Mark in 14: 64 (cf.

parallel in Matt. 26: 66). On balance the presence of ἐφάνη here cannot be said to lend any decisive weight either for or against Marcan authorship of this disputed section. Indeed virtually the same statement can be made about the whole phrase ἐφάνη πρῶτον Μαρίᾳ τῇ Μαγδαληνῇ.

παρά + genitive and ἐκβεβλήκει Although there is no exact parallel to παρ᾽ ἧς ἐκβεβλήκει ἑπτὰ δαιμόνια elsewhere in Mark, παρά with the genitive is found in Mk. 3: 21; 5: 26; 8: 11; 12: 2, 11; 14: 43, and ἐκβάλλω used with reference to casting out demons is usual for Mark (cf. Mk. 1: 34, 39; 3: 15, 22, 23; 6: 13; 7: 26; 9: 18, 28, 38). Certainly when compared to its Lucan parallel (Lk. 8: 2, ἀφ᾽ ἧς δαιμόνια ἑπτὰ ἐξεληλύθει), the phrasing at this point in Mk. 16: 9 can be said to be characteristically Marcan. *This means that taken as a whole, Mk. 16: 9 evidences that kind of stylistic affinity with the rest of Mark that would be expected were it to have been composed by the same writer responsible for Mk. 1: 1 – 16: 8.* This statement assumes that any verse taken at random from the text of Mark would probably exhibit some stylistic affinities with the text of Mark, while at the same time containing words and phrases which because of the rarity with which they are used or for some other equally valid reason could not be said to be typically Marcan. Such a verse taken at random would not be expected to exhibit characteristics distinctly atypical of Mark – and it is the absence of such negative stylistic phenomena in 16: 9 as well as the presence of phenomena commensurate with a stylistic kinship between this verse and the rest of Mark that justifies the italicized statement above.

Verse 10

ἐκείνη This word, used to mean 'that woman', is found elsewhere in the Gospels only in John (11: 29; 20: 15, 16); ἐκεῖνος used absolutely is found frequently in John chapters 10 through 20. Except for the last half of John, however, ἐκεῖνος used absolutely occurs infrequently in the Gospels. Interestingly enough the closest parallel to ἐκείνη πορευθεῖσα is found in John 20: 15, ἐκείνη δοκοῦσα, where we are struck by the fact that the woman concerned is precisely the same person, Mary Magdalene, and though the scene is different, Mary in both Mark and John is playing out a central role in the resurrection narrative. Were this the only linguistic kinship between Mk. 16: 10 and John 20: 11–18, it might be dismissed as a curious coincidence. However, John 20: 18 is parallel in other regards to Mk. 16: 10 as is indicated by the marginal cross-reference in Nestle. In both Mark and John, Mary Magdalene goes from the place where Jesus has appeared to her alone and reports to the disciples ('those who had been with him' according to Mark). This affinity between Mark and John is heightened by the fact that Mary Magdalene is not similarly singled out from the other women who went to the tomb in the resurrection narratives of either Matthew or Luke. The importance of this affinity between Mark and John cannot be clearly seen at this stage in our investigation. But we shall return to it at a later time. Meanwhile, it should be noted that ἐκεῖνος used absolutely is found not only here in verse 10 but also in verse 13 and verse 20, i.e. three times in these twelve verses. Since there is no comparable use of ἐκεῖνος elsewhere in Mark, this is evidence which supports the view that these verses are stylistically different from the rest of Mark. What the significance of this stylistic difference may be, whether it indicates a non-Marcan origin for these last twelve verses of Mark, must be decided after we have a more complete grasp of the totality of the linguistic phenomena involved.

πορευθεῖσα   The participial form of πορεύομαι occurs here in verse 10 and also in verses 12 and 15, and only once more in the entire Gospel of Mark, i.e. in 9: 30 where there is strong manuscript evidence for παραπορεύομαι. If the correct reading is παραπορεύομαι it may be said that the uncompounded form of πορεύομαι never occurs in Mark except in the last twelve verses, where it occurs three times and each time in the participial form. On the surface this would seem to be strong evidence for the stylistic unity of these verses and against their Marcan authorship. However, if we check to see what usage Mark exhibits in passages parallel to those in which Matthew and Luke employ πορεύομαι we discover that the use of πορεύομαι in 16: 9–20 does not argue against Marcan authorship as strongly as it appears to do at first sight. It can be shown that Mark has a preference for the compound forms of πορεύομαι, where some other construction using the uncompounded forms might as well have been used (Mk. 4: 19 seems to be a clear case in point). However, a compounded form of πορεύομαι in 16: 10 would have called for ἀποπορεύομαι which is a very rare word, never occurring in the New Testament or the LXX. In 16: 12 the participle πορευομένοις could not have been compounded with a preposition that would not have altered the meaning of the text. As will be noted in the treatment of verse 15, the un-compounded form of πορεύομαι in that verse is also used in the parallel passage in Matt. 28: 19, so that the appropriateness of its use in Mk. 16: 15 seems quite clear. Therefore, the use of πορεύομαι in Mk. 16: 9–20 does not represent strong evidence against Marcan authorship. Actually it has little probative value one way or the other for the question of the authenticity of these verses.

ἀπήγγειλεν This word which occurs again in 16: 13 is also found in Mk. 5: 14, 19 and 6: 30. By itself it tells us very little, except that it is in accord with Marcan usage.

τοῖς γενομένοις Though Mark uses γίνομαι frequently there is no other case when this particular use of γίνομαι is found in Mark. Once again, by itself this does not indicate anything very clearly about the relationship of Mk. 16: 9–20 to the rest of that Gospel. It certainly is not typical of Mark, but since many sentences in Mark would probably contain words or exhibit particular usages of some word which did not occur again in Mark, this kind of phenomenon tells us little if anything about the authorship of Mk. 16: 9–20, unless, of course, such *hapax legomena* prove to occur with unusual frequency.

τοῖς μετ᾽ αὐτοῦ This usage is found in Mk. 1: 36; 2: 25; 5: 40, as well as in Matt. 12: 3, 4; 26: 51; 27: 54, and Lk. 6: 3, 4, but nowhere else in the N.T.

τοῖς μετ᾽ αὐτοῦ γενομένοις This expression does not occur elsewhere in the N.T. But since οἱ μετ᾽ αὐτοῦ generally refers to persons who are with the person represented by the subject or the pronoun at the time of the action denoted by the main verb, whereas here the author is referring to those who were with Jesus at some time preceding the time Mary made her report to them, the use of the aorist participle of γίνομαι in this case is a simple modification of the phrase which makes clear that Mary made her report to those who 'had been with' Jesus.

πενθοῦσι καὶ κλαίουσιν This particular twofold combination is paralleled elsewhere in the Gospels only in Lk. 6: 25: οὐαί, οἱ γελῶντες νῦν, ὅτι πενθήσετε καὶ κλαύσετε. It occurs three times in Revelation, but in reverse order. It occurs in the same order in Jas. 4: 9 but in a threefold combination ταλαιπωρήσατε καὶ πενθήσατε καὶ κλαύσατε. πενθέω is not found elsewhere in Mark, but κλαίω is found in 5: 38, 39; and 14: 72. Unless this combination indicates some possible relationship between Mk. 16: 10 and the Gospel of Luke, there would seem to be little of importance in it for settling the question of the history of Mk. 16: 9–20. Because of the use of ἐκείνη and possibly πορευθεῖσα, verse 10, on balance, however slightly, seems to argue for non-Marcan authorship.

Verse 11

κἀκεῖνοι This word is used in a similar way here and also in 16: 13, i.e., to begin a subordinate sentence: κἀκεῖνοι ἀκούσαντες...κἀκεῖνοι ἀπελθόντες... It is also found in Mk. 12: 1–9 under similar circumstances: κἀκεῖνον ἐκεφαλαίωσαν...(12: 4); κἀκεῖνον ἀπέκτειναν...(12: 5). That κἀκεῖνον is followed by the participle here and in verse 13, and by the indicative in 12: 4, 5, is not so important. What is striking is that in the only two places in Mk. 1: 1 – 16: 20 where κἀκεῖνον is used, it is used in a combination of two adjoining compound sentences where it introduces the subordinate half of each sentence. In both chapter 12 and in chapter 16 the parallel structure of the sentence is further found to govern the syntax and grammar of the word immediately following. A comparison of Lk. 20: 11–12 // Mk. 12: 4–5 indicates that this is a syntactical peculiarity of Mark, and the fact that it is not found elsewhere in the N.T. lends added support to the view that Mark is probably responsible for the only other place in this Gospel where the same syntactical peculiarity is found – i.e. in 16: 11–13.

ἀκούσαντες This use of the participle of ἀκούω would not seem unnatural or unusual for Mark (cf. 2: 17; 3: 21; 6: 2, 29; 10: 41; 12: 28; 14: 11; 15: 35). For ἀκούσαντες ὅτι cf. 10: 47.

ζῆ   The use of 3άω here is altogether commensurate with Mark's use of it in 5: 23 and 12: 27, the only other places it occurs in his Gospel.

ἐθεάθη   This word which occurs here and again in 16: 14 is not found elsewhere in Mark. Since there are places where Mark might have used this word had he chosen to do so (Mk. 2: 14 and 15: 47), its occurrence twice in 16: 9–20 and not elsewhere in this Gospel points away from Marcan composition of 16: 11.

ὑπό + genitive   The use of ὑπό with the genitive is not unusual for Mark (cf. 1: 5, 9, 13; 2: 3; 5: 4, 26; 8: 31; 13: 13). However, this is a regular Greek construction and, therefore, neither confirms nor disputes Marcan usage.

ἠπίστησαν   This verb (ἀπιστέω) needs to be considered along with the adjective form ἄπιστος, and the noun form ἀπιστία. The following passages are relevant: 6: 6; 9: 19, 24; 16: 14, 16. In 6: 6 we find ἀπιστία; 9: 19 ἄπιστος; 9: 24 ἀπιστία; here, ἀπιστέω; 16: 14 ἀπιστία; 16: 16 ἀπιστέω. Matthew and Luke both use ἄπιστος; Matthew but not Luke uses ἀπιστία; Luke but not Matthew uses ἀπιστέω. The closest parallels to Mark's use of ἀπιστέω and ἀπιστία in 16: 9–20 are Luke's uses of ἀπιστέω in 24: 11 and 24: 41, where, as in Mk. 16: 9–20, there is a reference to the related disbelief of the disciples following the resurrection. For all practical purposes we can also include οὐκ ἐπίστευσαν in Mk. 16: 14 in our discussion at this point and conclude that there seems to be little if anything in all this that would significantly affect a judgment as to the history of Mk.16: 9–20, unless it would be to note the kinship between Mk. 16: 9–20 and the resurrection narrative in Lk. 24. But then it would be necessary to point out that the one time John uses any privative form of πιστός, πιστίς or πιστεύω is in 20: 27 where with reference to the doubt of Thomas (οὐ μὴ πιστεύσω 20: 25) Jesus says: 'do not be faithless but believing (μὴ γίνου ἄπιστος ἀλλὰ πιστός)'. The effect of all this would be to emphasize the point that there is no linguistic ground for separating Mk. 16: 9–20 from the rest of Mark on the basis of the use made of the privative forms of πιστός, πιστίς or πιστεύω. For if John could restrict his use of the privative of πιστός to his resurrection narrative, Mark could, with no more cause for question, similarly restrict his use of the privative of πιστεύω.

This analysis shows that on balance the evidence weighs more in favour of regarding Mk. 16: 11 as being from the same hand responsible for Mk. 1: 1 – 16: 8, than it is in favour of regarding this verse as from a different hand. This is because the syntactical evidence concerning the use of κἀκεῖνος would seem to outweigh the linguistic evidence concerning the use of θεάομαι.

Verse 12

Μετὰ δὲ ταῦτα This expression is found frequently in Luke, John and Revelation, but not at all in Matthew and only this one time in Mark. On the other hand μετά with the accusative followed by a sequential infinitive, which occurs in Mk. 16: 19 and provides the only other use of μετά with the accusative in Mk. 16: 9–20, is found in Mk. 1: 14 and 14: 28. It is found only once in Matt. (26: 32 // Mk. 14: 28), twice in Lk. (12: 5; 22: 20) and not at all in John. In other words μετὰ δὲ ταῦτα (or μετὰ ταῦτα), found fairly frequently elsewhere in the N.T., is found in Mark only in 16: 9–20, indicating a dissimilarity between these verses and the rest of Mark. However, μετά with the sequential infinitive which occurs more rarely elsewhere in the N.T. is found once in 16: 9–20 and twice elsewhere in Mark, indicating a grammatical kinship between these last verses of Mark and the rest of the Gospel. The phenomenon of the single appearance of one particular use of μετά with the accusative in the whole text of a Gospel is not unique – cf. Matthew's single use of μετά and sequential infinitive in 26: 32. Therefore, it is difficult to place much if any weight on the single occurrence of μετὰ δὲ ταῦτα here in the whole text of Mark. But when one considers that μετά with sequential infinitive occurs as often in Mark as in Matthew, Luke and John together, it appears that this usage is at least slightly distinctive of Mark. Because it occurs infrequently even in Mark, it cannot be argued that this constitutes evidence indicating Marcan authorship for 16: 9–20. However, it easily counterbalances any suggestion based on the presence here of μετὰ δὲ ταῦτα that 16: 9–20 is non-Marcan in origin.

δυσὶν ἐξ αὐτῶν   This expression has its closest parallel in Lk. 24: 13 where the same use is made of it. The fact that the exact phrase does not occur elsewhere in the N.T. is probably no more than a coincidence. But that this phrase occurs only in these two passages and that in both cases it refers to two disciples who, after hearing a post-resurrection report they would not believe, themselves were made witnesses to the resurrected Jesus while walking along together – this is a rather striking indication of some kind of literary relationship between Lk. 24: 13 and Mk. 16: 12. In any case the presence of this expression (which does not occur elsewhere in Mark) in Mk. 16: 9–20 is no more evidence that these verses did not belong to the autograph of Mark than its presence in Lk. 24: 13 is evidence that Lk. 24: 13–53 did not belong to the autograph of Luke.

περιπατοῦσιν   There is nothing unusual about Mark's use of περιπατέω. He uses it with about the same frequency and range of meanings as most of the other N.T. writers.

ἐφανερώθη   This exact form occurs also in Mk. 16: 14. Since φανερόω occurs also in Mk. 4: 22 and φανερός in 3: 12; 4: 22; and 6: 14 and φανερῶς in 1: 45, and since φανερόω, used by John several times, is used by him in exactly the same form in his resurrection narrative (John 21: 14), there seems to be nothing unusual in Mark's use of the word here and in 16: 14, and there certainly is no cause to think that the use of φανερόω here argues for a non-Marcan origin for Mk. 16: 9–20.

ἐν ἑτέρᾳ μορφῇ   ἕτερος and ἄλλος can sometimes be interchanged, and in such cases Mark seems to prefer ἄλλος (cf. Mk. 4: 5, 7, 8; 8: 28; 12: 4). However, ἄλλος generally refers to *other* or *another* when more than two are involved. ὁ ἄλλος can mean *the other* of two only. ἕτερος is sometimes used to mean *another*, or a *second* of two, and sometimes of more than two to mean *other* or *different*. Whether ἄλλος could have been used equally well here in place of ἕτερος is not clear. The matter is further complicated by the fact that it is not clear whether the meaning is that Jesus appeared in a form different from that in which he appeared to Mary Magdalene (could the use of φαίνω (16: 9) rather than φανερόω lend support to such a view?), or merely that it was another form from that in which they had seen him last. If ἄλλος could have been used to mean what ἕτε-ρος was here intended to mean, then the use of ἕτερος here would argue against considering Mk. 16: 9–20 as from the same hand as Mk. 1: 1 – 16: 8, for elsewhere in Mark ἄλλος is consistently used where ἕτερος is found in a parallel passage in either Matthew or Luke.

μορφῇ This word is used elsewhere in the N.T. only in Phil. 2: 6, and 2: 7. Since it is used in Mk. 16: 12 in reference to an explicit post-resurrection appearance of Jesus, there is no reason to be surprised that it does not appear elsewhere in the text of Mark. That this word appears elsewhere in the N.T. only in a Christological passage preserved in a letter of Paul is intriguing, but seems to throw no clear light on the history of Mk. 16: 9–20, and certainly none on whether these verses belong to the auto-graph of the Gospel.

πορευομένοις εἰς ἀγρόν πορευομένοις has been discussed with reference to πορευθεῖσα in verse 10. ἀγρός used in this sense to mean 'into the country' is peculiar to Mark among N.T. writers – cf. Mk. 15: 21 where ἐρχόμενον ἀπ' ἀγροῦ should be translated: 'coming in from the country'.

πορευομένοις εἰς ἀγρόν then, generally translated 'going into the country', turns out to have its closest linguistic kinship in the N.T. with Mk. 15: 21 which by itself argues for regarding 16: 9–20 as belonging with Mk. 1: 1 – 16: 8 (cf. also Mk. 13: 16).

On balance, verse 12 seems quite problematic. Neither the evidence for nor that against Marcan authorship seems to be very strong.

Verse 13

κἀκεῖνοι Cf. verse 11 above.

ἀπελθόντες Mark uses ἀπέρχομαι frequently and this exact form in 6: 36, 37 and 4: 12. There seems to be nothing unusual in its use here.

ἀπήγγειλαν Cf. verse 10.

τοῖς λοιποῖς There seems to be nothing unusual in the use of this expression.

οὐδέ   Nor of this.

ἐκείνοις   See verse 10.

ἐπίστευσαν   Cf. 16: 14 where the same word is used in the same way. Mark uses πιστεύω fairly often and in ways quite comparable to its use in 16: 9–20 (cf. 11: 31; 13: 21).

Verse 14

Ὕστερον   This is found only here in Mark. Though used several times in Matthew, it is found only once in Luke, once in John and once in Hebrews. Therefore, its presence only once in Mark affords little or no basis for a judgment concerning authorship.

ἀνακειμένοις   This word is used in the N.T. only in the Gospels, but in Mark with about the same frequency as in the other three Gospels and in the same way and with practically the same meaning. Cf. Mk. 6: 26; and 14: 18.

ἕνδεκα   This word is a technical term which refers to the 'twelve' minus Judas Iscariot, and in the Gospels occurs only in the post-resurrection narratives: Matt. 28: 16; Mk. 16: 14; Lk. 24: 9, 33. It occurs also in Acts 1: 26, and 2: 14. Its presence here is perfectly natural and its absence elsewhere in Mark occasions no surprise. Indeed its presence elsewhere in Mark would be anomalous.

ἐφανερώθη   Cf. verse 12.

ὠνείδισεν   Mark uses this word in 15: 32, 34. Matthew uses it three times, Luke once and John not at all.

τὴν ἀπιστίαν   Cf. verse 11 ἠπίστησαν.

σκληροκαρδίαν   This word occurs only three times in the N.T.: Matt. 19: 8 // Mk. 10: 5 and here.

ὅτι   Mark usually uses a post-positive γάρ to introduce an explanatory phrase. But he also uses a causal ὅτι, as here, frequently.

θεασαμένοις   Cf. verse 11.

ἐγηγερμένον Mark several times uses this word in the same sense as here – i.e. for the resurrection (cf. 6: 14, 16; 12: 26; 14: 28; 16: 6).

Verse 15

καὶ εἶπεν αὐτοῖς Mark has no exact parallel to this. But neither is there anything particularly noteworthy. All constituent parts are common enough in Mark.

πορευθέντες Cf. verse 10. The nearest parallel to this particular use of the participle of πορεύομαι as an imperative is found in the closely related exhortation in Matt. 28: 19.

ἅπαντα Mark uses this word in 1: 27; 8: 25; 11: 32. Its use here calls for no special comment.

τὸν κόσμον κόσμος is found in Mk. 8: 36 and 14: 9. The expression εἰς τὸν κόσμον ἅπαντα κηρύξατε τὸ εὐαγγέλιον finds its nearest parallel in Mk. 14: 9: κηρυχθῇ τὸ εὐαγγέλιον εἰς ὅλον τὸν κόσμον (//Matt. 26: 13).

τὸ εὐαγγέλιον Paul frequently uses εὐαγγέλιον absolutely; though he also uses 'my' gospel, 'our' gospel, the Gospel 'of God', and the Gospel of Christ, etc. Mark once has the Gospel of Jesus Christ (1: 1), and once the Gospel of God (1: 14). But elsewhere it is always simply 'the Gospel', used, as in Paul, absolute (cf. 1: 15; 8: 35; 10: 29; 13: 10; 14: 9). This is distinctive of Mark among the evangelists, and is one of the striking linguistic and conceptual affinities between Mark and Paul. Matthew never uses the expression; nor does John. Luke never uses it though it occurs once in Acts 15: 7. The presence here of τὸ εὐαγγέλιον, used absolutely, constitutes a strong linguistic tie between Mk. 1: 1 – 16: 8 and 16: 9–20.

If all the resurrection narratives were separated from the Gospels and someone unacquainted with the Gospels were asked to attempt to rematch each Gospel with its proper concluding section, the presence of τὸ εὐαγγέλιον used absolutely in Mk. 16: 9–20 would provide an unmistakable key to the mystery: to which of the four Gospels do these verses belong? On the basis of this consideration, they could only be joined to Mark.

πάσῃ   This use of πᾶς is common in Mark and in the N.T. as a whole. It calls for no special comment.

πάσῃ τῇ κτίσει   κτίσις is found also in Mk. 10: 6, and 13: 19. It is not found in the other Gospels or Acts, but it occurs eleven times in Paul and five times in the rest of the N.T. literature. The nearest parallel seems to be in Col. 1: 23 where πᾶσα κτίσις is used in the dative as here in Mark to suggest the extent or limits to which the Gospel is to be preached.

On the usual view that verse 15 was composed after the other gospels were written this verse would appear to be a composition in which the great command of the Risen Lord in Matt. 28: 19 has been modified under the influence of the teaching of the Risen Lord in Lk. 24: 47 where in place of an emphasis on 'teaching πάντα τὰ ἔθνη to keep all that Jesus commanded', there is an emphasis on 'preaching repentance and forgiveness of sins to πάντα τὰ ἔθνη'. One would see also the influence of the formulation of Jesus in Matt. 26: 13 // Mk. 14: 9 where 'preaching the gospel to the whole κόσμος' is mentioned. That verse 15 is distinctively Marcan, however, is strongly supported by the presence in Mk. 13: 10 of the unique Marcan formulation: καὶ εἰς πάντα τὰ ἔθνη πρῶτον δεῖ κηρυχθῆναι τὸ εὐαγγέλιον, which in turn exhibits Pauline features in comparison with its parallel in Matt. 24: 14, where instead of the simple predictive future of κηρύσσω ('This gospel of the Kingdom *will be preached* in the whole inhabited world as a witness to all the Gentiles'), Mark has 'First it is *necessary that* "the Gospel" *be preached* to all the Gentiles.' This formulation is commensurate with the understanding of the purpose of the preaching to the Gentiles expressed by Paul in Rom. 10–11 where all men (πάντες) are the ultimate object of God's mercy (both Jew and Gentile, cf. 11: 32–6), and where the reconciliation of the κόσμος is in view (cf. 11: 15), but where *preaching* 'the Gospel' is essential to God's purpose of saving everyone (πᾶς, cf. 10: 13ff.), and where the mission to the Gentiles (τὰ ἔθνη, cf. 11: 11, 12, 13, 25) must be completed before Israel will be saved (cf. 11: 11–12 and 25–6). The point is that in Mark the apocalyptic discourse has been modified to make clear that the consummation at the end of the age spoken of therein will not take place until 'the Gospel' has been preached to πάντα τὰ ἔθνη. Such a notion places a cosmic significance upon the mission to the Gentiles that finds its fullest expression in the N.T. in Rom. 10–11, and thus unites Mark to Paul in this special connection. Mk. 16: 15 is similarly Pauline in its emphasis upon the 'cosmos' and the 'whole of creation' and its concept of the 'preaching of the Gospel'. As is clear from Rom. 10–11, and Col. 1: 23, κόσμος and πᾶσα ἡ κτίσις are concepts more unambiguously inclusive than πάντα τὰ ἔθνη. For πάντα τὰ ἔθνη could be taken as all the nations exclusive of Israel – i.e. 'the Gentiles', so Paul frequently (cf. Rom. 11: 11–12), whereas κόσμος and πᾶσα ἡ κτίσις included 'all men' inclusive of Israel. Mark's use of τὰ ἔθνη in 13: 10 is perfectly in keeping with the technical use of τὰ ἔθνη in Rom. 11: 11–12 (i.e. the nations exclusive of Israel), but in Mk. 16: 15 any writer, whether Mark or some one else, if he were to do justice to the universal implications of πάντα τὰ ἔθνη in Matt. 28: 19, and/or Lk. 24: 47, and if he were to give full expression to the universalism in Rom. 10–11, would be led to use the unambiguously inclusive concepts of κόσμος and πᾶσα ἡ κτίσις where πάντα τὰ ἔθνη stood in the corresponding words of the Risen Lord in Matthew and Luke.

There seems to be nothing in Mk. 16: 15 that is non-Marcan, and there is much that suggests for it 'Marcan' authorship with a concern to represent the intentions of the Son of God in terms that are as faithful as possible to the sometimes common but sometimes divergent accounts of Matthew and Luke, all under the influence of concepts that seem to be distinctively Pauline.

Verse 16

ὁ πιστεύσας Cf. Mk. 9: 23, 42, as well as 16: 17 where there is a similar use of the participial form of πιστεύω.

βαπτισθείς Nothing unusual.

σωθήσεται Nothing unusual.

ἀπιστήσας Cf. verse 11.

κατακριθήσεται Mark uses κατακρίνω in 10: 33 and 14: 64. It occurs four times in Matthew, twice in Luke. On all of verse 16 see John 3: 18.

Verse 17

σημεῖα occurs also in verse 20. It is not unusual in Mark. Cf. Mk. 8: 11, 12; 13: 4, 22. See discussion of σημείων in verse 20.

παρακολουθήσει occurs only here in Mark. But it occurs only once in Luke (1: 3) and once in 1 Tim. (4: 6) and once in 2 Tim. (3: 10). Its presence this once in Mark calls for no special comment.

ἐν τῷ ὀνόματί μου δαιμόνια ἐκβαλοῦσιν (cf. Acts 4: 30) Elsewhere Mark uses ἐπί rather than ἐν to introduce the expression τῷ ὀνόματί μου, cf. 9: 37, 39, and 13: 6. However, he uses ἐν to introduce a closely related expression in a similar phrase, cf. ἐν τῷ ὀνόματί σου ἐκβάλλοντα δαιμόνια Mk. 9: 38.

γλώσσαις λαλήσουσιν καιναῖς The expression 'to speak in tongues' is found in Acts and Paul numerous times. But 'to speak in *new* tongues' is found only here in the N.T.

Verse 18

ὄφεις There is nothing unusual about this word, and its use here is fitting for the context.

ἀροῦσιν Mark uses this word frequently. There is no true parallel to 'picking up serpents' in the N.T. But the promise to the faithful that they would be enabled to tread on serpents is made in Ps. 91: 13, and seems to be reflected in the similar promise to the seventy in Lk. 14: 15, where it is explicitly said, as here (though not in the same words), that this would be done with impunity.

κἄν Mark uses this (5: 28 and 6: 56) with a frequency more or less comparable to the other evangelists.

θανάσιμον This word never occurs elsewhere in the N.T. or in any of the Greek translations of the O.T., including the Apocrypha. There is no other place in Mark where the evangelist had occasion to use this rare word.

τι Mark uses τις relatively often, and in a conditional construction with εἰ or ἐάν with an even greater relative frequency. However, elsewhere in Mark τις is never separated from the conditional particle as here. This by itself seems to weigh against common authorship of this verse and Mk. 1: 1 – 16: 8. However, such a separation occurs rarely in the other Gospels, and when it does, as in Matt. 18: 12, it is not regarded as evidence that that verse did not belong to the autograph of Matthew, but that the evangelist was copying a source.

πίωσιν   Nothing unusual.

οὐ μή   This is a most interesting phenomenon. This construction is somewhat rare in the N.T., especially so in Luke–Acts and Mark. It is used in Lk. 10: 19, and in Mark, besides 16: 18, only in 13: 2, 19, 30. This is a relatively rare construction whose distribution in the synoptic gospels is of interest. For Lk. 10: 19 is the same passage which we have already seen to be the closest synoptic parallel to Mk. 16: 18. Both by content and by this linguistic construction Lk. 10: 19 is tied to Mk. 16: 18. The presumption would seem to be that whoever composed Mk. 16: 18 has been influenced by Lk. 10: 19. But was that the evangelist Mark? It would seem so, for the following reason: we have noted that the only other occurrences of this construction in Mark are found in Mk. 13. This Marcan apocalypse has a very close parallel in Matt. 24 where the same construction occurs in the parallel passages. The presence of ἦν ἔκτισεν ὁ θεός in Mk. 13: 19 is to be regarded as a dogmatic gloss on the more original text as represented by Matt. 24: 19. Therefore, Mk. 13: 19 is either secondary to Matt. 24: 21 or secondary to a source common to Matthew and Mark. The presence of the unusual construction οὐ μή in Mk. 13: 19, also found in Matt. 24: 21, is thus best accounted for by the hypothesis of copying. This means that as far as Mark is concerned the presence of this construction in 13: 19 is best accounted for on the assumption that it has come into the text of Mark through the process of his copying a source where it was present. Whether this source was Matthew or some other source is immaterial at this point. But once this is recognized, the presence of the same construction here under similar circumstances is striking. It seems that in both cases we have Mark using a relatively rare construction because it is in the source upon which he is dependent. It should be emphasized that the expression does not seem to be characteristic of Mark's style. However, its presence in Mk. 13 and in 16: 9–20 under similar redactional circumstances suggests a linguistic tie between these two sections, and on balance argues for a common redactional origin, i.e. from the hand of the evangelist.

βλάψη This word occurs elsewhere in the N.T. only in Lk. 4: 35·

ἐπὶ ἀρρώστους χεῖρας ἐπιθήσουσιν καὶ καλῶς ἕξουσιν Mark uses ἐπιτίθημι several times, and generally in connection with χείρ (cf. Mk. 5: 23; 6: 5; 7: 32; 8: 23, 25). The indirect object is generally placed in the simple dative case without the preposition ἐπί as in the otherwise closely parallel ἀρρώστοις ἐπιθεὶς τὰς χεῖρας (Mk. 6: 5). But Mark can also repeat the preposition ἐπί and use the accusative case as in 8: 25 ἐπέθηκεν τὰς χεῖρας ἐπὶ τοὺς ὀφθαλμούς.

The concept of 'laying on of hands' for blessing, healing, receiving the Holy Spirit or ordaining, never found in John or Paul (once in 1 Timothy), is found more frequently in Acts and Mark than in any other books of the N.T.

ἀρρώστους seems to be the word for diseases Mark prefers in similar contexts, cf. Mk. 6: 5, 13. Matthew seems to prefer νόσος and μαλακία in such contexts. Cf. Matt. 4: 23; 9: 35; 10: 1. Mark uses νόσος once (Mk. 1: 34).

καλῶς ἕξουσιν καλῶς ἔχειν occurs only here in the N.T. But καλῶς is used by Mark in 7: 6, 9, 37; 12: 28, 32. And καὶ καλῶς ἕξουσιν contrasts well with the only other use in Mark of ἔχειν in an adverbial construction (i.e. with κακῶς 1: 32, 34; 2: 17; 6: 55) where it is used as here in contexts of healing.

In summary there seems to be no reason to regard this compound phrase as non-Marcan. On the side of Marcan authorship the use of ἀρρώστους constitutes a tenuous, but not insignificant, linguistic tie between Mk. 1: 1 – 16: 8 and 16: 9–20. The fact that Mark uses the concept of 'laying on of hands' more frequently than do any of the other evangelists points to the same conclusion.

Ὁ μὲν οὖν κύριος ὁ κύριος to refer to Jesus does not occur elsewhere in Mark, nor does the construction μὲν οὖν. However, the latter occurs only once in Luke (3: 18), in what appears to be a redactional section from the hand of the evangelist himself, and the former, possibly foreshadowed by allusion in Mk. 9: 19, would not be wrongly reserved to be used as a title befitting the resurrected and ascended Jesus. However, in order that we do not overlook or minimize evidence let us remand this phrase as possibly non-Marcan.

Verse 19

μετὰ τὸ λαλῆσαι αὐτοῖς   Mark uses μετά with the accusative several times and twice in a sequential infinitive construction (1: 14; 14: 28). Mark uses λαλέω several times, usually placing its object, when it is a personal pronoun, in the dative case. The dative plural αὐτοῖς seems to be characteristic of Mark. The remainder of verse 19 is taken from 2 Kings 2: 11 and Ps. 110: 1.

Verse 20

ἐκεῖνοι   Beginning a sentence with ἐκεῖνοι with a postpositive δέ is found in Mk. 12: 7 where the construction is peculiar to Mark in comparison to the parallel texts of Matthew and Luke.

ἐξελθόντες   Mark uses the participial form of ἐξέρχομαι fairly often and in 6: 12 in a redactional passage we have ἐξελθόντες ἐκήρυξαν as here, *and in a similar context.*

πανταχοῦ   This rather rare word, which does not occur in either Matthew or John, is found once in Luke (5: 6) but also in Mk. 1: 28. ἐκεῖνοι δὲ ἐξελθόντες ἐκήρυξαν πανταχοῦ could be a Marcan construction.

τοῦ κυρίου συνεργοῦντος   συνεργέω and the related word συνεργός are relatively rare words in hellenistic Greek. Paul is their principal New Testament user. The use of the word here may reflect Pauline influence.

τὸν λόγον βεβαιοῦντος   In Matt. 13: 19 the seed in the parable of the Sower is explained as representing 'the Word of the Kingdom'. In Lk. 8: 11 it is 'the Word of God'. In Mk. 4: 15 it is simply 'the Word' – used absolutely. Mark never uses the expressions 'the Word of the Kingdom' or 'the Word of God'. For this concept he always uses the simple absolute construction: 'the Word'. The relevant passages are Mk. 1: 45;

2: 2; 4: 33; 8: 32; 9: 10; [16: 20]. In 4: 33 there can be no doubt that he is using ὁ λόγος in the same technical sense that elsewhere Luke uses ὁ λόγος τοῦ θεοῦ and Matthew uses ὁ λόγος τῆς βασιλείας. The first time Mark uses the expression (Mk. 1: 45) it is possible to take it in a non-technical sense as many translators since Tyndale have done. But in Mk. 2: 2 it clearly seems to be used in a sense equivalent to Luke's 'the Word of God', although it is by no means clear what Mark has in mind for the reader to understand by the expression at that point. The first hint that for Mark the expression has reference to the resurrection is given in 8: 32 when after Jesus is represented as predicting his passion and resurrection the text reads: καὶ παρρησίᾳ τὸν λόγον ἐλάλει which although it can be rendered as a kind of innocuous gloss 'and he said this plainly', according to close parallels (John 7: 26; 18: 20; Acts 4: 31; 28: 31), should be rendered 'and he spoke the Word openly'.

This connection of 'the Word' with the resurrection seems clear in Mk. 9: 10. Peter, James and John have witnessed the transfiguration of Jesus and have been told not to tell anyone what they had seen 'until the Son of Man was risen from the dead'. Then the text reads: καὶ τὸν λόγον ἐκράτησαν πρὸς ἑαυτοὺς συζητοῦντες τί ἐστιν τὸ ἐκ νεκρῶν ἀναστῆναι, which can fairly be rendered: 'and they kept the Word to themselves – questioning what it meant "to be raised from the dead"'. Here 'the Word' seems to refer to the resurrection of the Son of Man. It is this they were not to tell, it was this they kept to themselves, and it was this whose meaning they pondered.

In verse 20 we learn that those who had witnessed the resurrected Jesus, following his ascension, 'went out and preached everywhere' (just as Jesus at the beginning of his ministry 'went out and preached many things'), Jesus (as ὁ κύριος) working with them and confirming the Word by the accompanying signs (cf. Acts 14: 3). That is, similar mighty works which accompanied Jesus' preaching before his death now accompany the preaching of the disciples after his death because of the resurrection which has made possible the presence of the Risen Lord with the disciples. And it may be said that these σημεῖα confirm τὸν λόγον since ὁ γόλος is the message of the resurrection of the Son of Man, and the continuation of mighty works like those Jesus performed before his death, after his death, can only mean that he is not dead but lives – i.e. as the resurrected and ascended Lord of the disciples. The parallel between Mk. 1: 45 and 16: 20 is in substance striking: Jesus '*going out* began to *preach* many things and to *spread the Word* (1: 45)'; the disciples who had seen the resurrected Jesus, '*going out preached* everywhere, the Lord working with them and *confirming the Word*'. The use of τὸν λόγον absolutely in verse 20 is a strong linguistic and conceptual tie uniting Mk. 16: 9–20 with the rest of the text of Mark. The occurrence of this phrase in a sentence featuring the activity of preaching suggests that verse 20 has come from the same redactional hand responsible for Mk. 1: 45.

There is an intelligible development in the use of ὁ λόγος throughout Mark. And 16: 20 is in keeping with that development, and indeed offers a fitting climax to it.

βεβαιοῦντος This word, like συνεργέω, is used by Paul more often than all the other New Testament writers together. It does not occur elsewhere in any of the Gospels or in Acts. It is perfectly suitable to the context – and like συνεργέω could owe its presence here to Pauline influence. There is no parallel in the N.T. to the use of the verb form βεβαιόω for the confirming of ὁ λόγος. But βέβαιος is so used in Heb. 2: 2 and 2 Pet. 1: 19.

Since Mark is sometimes characterized by having concepts and vocabulary close to Paul, the use of these two Pauline words in Mk. 16: 20, on balance, at least as far as this consideration is concerned, presents no difficulty for regarding Mk. 16: 9–20 as Marcan.

τῶν ἐπακολουθούντων This is another word found relatively infrequently in the N.T. (1 Tim. 5: 10, 24; 1 Pet. 2: 21). It fits the context well here, however, and since it never occurs in the other Gospels, it is impossible to make a judgment as to whether on balance this word weighs for or against Marcan authorship for 16: 9–20.

σημείων The use of a compound form of ἀκολουθέω referring to σημεῖα is found in 16: 17 as well as here. In both cases the reference is to the signs mentioned in 16: 17b–18. These signs confirm the message preached after the resurrection and accompany the faithful in the post-resurrection community. They are not to be confused with the σημεῖα demanded of Jesus by the scribes and Pharisees – which he refused to perform, according to Matthew, Mark and Luke. They find their true parallel in Acts 14: 3 where, as here, ὁ κύριος, working through apostles, bears witness to 'the Word' of his grace by granting σημεῖα and wonders through their hands.

This completes a survey of the relevant linguistic data bearing on the question of Marcan authorship of the last twelve verses of Mark. Evidence for non-Marcan authorship seems to be preponderant in verse 10. Verses 12, 14, 16, 17, 18, and 19 seem to be either basically, or in balance, neutral. Evidence for Marcan authorship seems to be preponderant in verses 9, 11, 13, 15, and 20.

The connection between verse 8 and verses 9–20 appears to some to be so awkward that it is difficult to believe that the evangelist intended verses 9–20 to be a continuation of the Gospel. The awkwardness chiefly consists in (a) the change in subject between verses 8 and 9, (b) the identification of Mary Magdalene though she has been mentioned previously in 15: 47 and 16: 1. The change in subject between verses 8 and 9 would occasion no comment were it not that Jesus as the subject of verse 9 is unexpressed. It is difficult to assess the force of this circumstance. The identification of Mary Magdalene though she has been mentioned twice previously is paralleled by the Marcan use of αὐτή in 14: 54 and 14: 66 without identification and then in 15: 16 with the addition of ὅ ἐστιν πραιτώριον. Abrupt transitions are not unusual in Mark, and such awkwardness as may exist remains whether the evangelist or some later person added the verses concerned.